Hong Kong

Everything You Need to Know

Copyright © 2024 by Noah Gil-Smith.

All rights reserved. No part of this book may be reproduced, distributed, or transmitted in any form or by any means, including photocopying, recording, or other electronic or mechanical methods, without the prior written permission of the publisher, except in the case of brief quotations embodied in critical reviews and certain other noncommercial uses permitted by copyright law. This book was created with the assistance of Artificial Intelligence. The content presented in this book is for entertainment purposes only. It should not be considered as a substitute for professional advice or comprehensive research. Readers are encouraged to independently verify any information and consult relevant experts for specific matters. The author and publisher disclaim any liability or responsibility for any loss, injury, or inconvenience caused or alleged to be caused directly or indirectly by the information presented in this book.

Introduction to Hong Kong 6

A Brief History of Hong Kong: From Fishing Villages to Global Metropolis 8

Colonial Legacy: Hong Kong under British Rule 10

Return to China: The Handover and Its Implications 12

Governance and Politics: One Country, Two Systems 15

Economic Powerhouse: Hong Kong as a Financial Hub 18

Skyscrapers and Skyline: The Architectural Marvels 21

Natural Wonders: Exploring Hong Kong's Wildlife and Parks 23

From Dim Sum to Michelin Stars: A Culinary Journey 25

Tea Culture: Tradition in Every Sip 28

Must-Visit Markets: Shopping Extravaganza 30

Iconic Landmarks: Exploring Hong Kong's Tourist Sights 32

Hong Kong Disneyland: Where Magic Meets the East 34

Lantau Island: Nature, Spirituality, and the Big Buddha 37

Kowloon: A Fusion of Old and New 39

The New Territories: Exploring Hong Kong's Countryside 41

Macau: The Vegas of the East 43

Colonial Charm: Historic Buildings and Neighborhoods 45

Victoria Harbour: The Heartbeat of Hong Kong 47

Avenue of Stars: Honoring Hong Kong's Film Industry 49

Festivals and Celebrations: Colorful Traditions 51

The Art Scene: Creativity in Every Corner 53

Mahjong and Tai Chi: Traditional Pastimes 55

Cantonese Opera: A Theatrical Heritage 57

Feng Shui: Harmony in Design and Life 60

Chinese New Year: The Biggest Celebration 62

Dragon Boat Festival: Racing on the Water 64

Mid-Autumn Festival: Mooncakes and Lanterns 66

Ghost Festival: Honoring the Ancestors 68

Language and Linguistic Diversity: Cantonese and Beyond 70

Learning Cantonese: Essential Phrases and Etiquette 73

English in Hong Kong: Language of Business and Administration 76

Religion and Belief Systems: Temples, Churches, and Mosques 79

Buddhism: Temples and Practices 82

Taoism: Influence on Everyday Life 85

Christianity: Historical and Contemporary Presence 88

Islam: Hong Kong's Muslim Community 91

Education System: From Kindergarten to University 94

Healthcare System: Access and Quality of Care 97

Transportation: Navigating the Urban Jungle 100

Public Transit: Efficient and Extensive 102

The Tramways: A Nostalgic Ride 105

Green Initiatives: Sustainability Efforts 107

Epilogue 110

Introduction to Hong Kong

Hong Kong, a dynamic city on the southeastern coast of China, is a captivating fusion of East and West, where ancient traditions meet modern innovation. Nestled on the Pearl River Delta and flanked by the South China Sea, this bustling metropolis is a vibrant tapestry of cultures, languages, and lifestyles.

With a rich history dating back thousands of years, Hong Kong's story is one of resilience, adaptation, and transformation. From its humble beginnings as a collection of fishing villages to its rise as a global economic powerhouse, Hong Kong's journey is nothing short of remarkable. Its strategic location has made it a coveted territory throughout history, attracting merchants, adventurers, and conquerors alike.

The British colonization in the 19th century left an indelible mark on Hong Kong, shaping its governance, architecture, and culture. For over 150 years, Hong Kong thrived under British rule, evolving into a thriving international trade hub and financial center. The iconic Victoria Harbour, with its stunning skyline punctuated by skyscrapers, stands as a testament to the city's growth and prosperity during this period.

In 1997, Hong Kong underwent a historic transition as sovereignty was transferred from Britain to China. The "one country, two systems" framework was established, granting Hong Kong a high degree of autonomy within the People's Republic of China. This unique arrangement has allowed Hong Kong to maintain its distinct identity while fostering closer ties with mainland China.

Today, Hong Kong is a bustling cosmopolitan city renowned for its efficiency, innovation, and cultural diversity. Its bustling streets are lined with bustling street markets, luxury boutiques, and Michelin-starred restaurants, offering a sensory feast for visitors and locals alike. From the tranquil beauty of its parks and nature reserves to the excitement of its world-class entertainment and nightlife, Hong Kong offers something for everyone.

But beyond its glitzy facade lies a city with a rich cultural heritage and a deep sense of tradition. Temples, shrines, and historic buildings coexist harmoniously with sleek skyscrapers, reflecting Hong Kong's blend of old and new. Its festivals, from Chinese New Year to the Mid-Autumn Festival, are vibrant celebrations of its multicultural identity, drawing people from around the world to join in the festivities.

As we delve deeper into the heart of Hong Kong, we will explore its history, its people, its cuisine, and its unique way of life. From the bustling streets of Central to the tranquil beaches of Lantau Island, join us on a journey through this extraordinary city where East meets West and tradition meets innovation. Welcome to Hong Kong, where every corner tells a story and every moment is an adventure.

A Brief History of Hong Kong: From Fishing Villages to Global Metropolis

Hong Kong's history is a tapestry woven with threads of resilience, adaptation, and transformation. Long before the gleaming skyscrapers and bustling streets, Hong Kong was a humble collection of fishing villages nestled along the rugged coastline of southeastern China. Its earliest inhabitants were the Tanka people, who built their homes on stilts above the waters of the Pearl River Delta.

In the 19th century, Hong Kong's strategic location caught the attention of British traders seeking to expand their influence in the region. In 1841, following the First Opium War, the Qing Dynasty ceded Hong Kong Island to Britain under the Treaty of Nanking. The island's deep natural harbor, now known as Victoria Harbour, provided an ideal port for British ships engaged in trade with China.

Under British rule, Hong Kong underwent rapid development and urbanization. The construction of roads, railways, and infrastructure transformed the landscape, while the influx of immigrants from China and other parts of Asia fueled the city's growth. By the late 19th century, Hong Kong had emerged as a major center of commerce, attracting merchants, traders, and entrepreneurs from around the world.

The 20th century brought both prosperity and challenges to Hong Kong. The city weathered economic downturns, political unrest, and two world wars, yet continued to thrive as a vital hub of trade and finance in the Asia-Pacific region. The post-war years saw a surge in industrialization, as Hong Kong's manufacturing sector boomed, producing textiles, electronics, and other goods for export.

In 1997, Hong Kong underwent a historic transition as sovereignty was transferred from Britain to China. The "one country, two systems" framework was established, granting Hong Kong a high degree of autonomy within the People's Republic of China. Despite initial concerns about its future, Hong Kong's status as a global financial center and gateway to China remained intact, ensuring its continued relevance on the world stage.

Since the handover, Hong Kong has experienced rapid modernization and economic growth, fueled by its status as a global financial hub and center for trade and commerce. The city's skyline has been transformed by gleaming skyscrapers, while its cultural landscape has evolved to reflect its diverse population and cosmopolitan outlook.

Today, Hong Kong stands as a shining example of East-meets-West, where tradition and modernity coexist harmoniously. Its bustling streets are a testament to its vibrant energy and entrepreneurial spirit, while its cultural heritage is preserved in its temples, shrines, and historic landmarks. As we delve deeper into Hong Kong's history, we will uncover the stories of resilience, ingenuity, and perseverance that have shaped this remarkable city into the global metropolis it is today.

Colonial Legacy: Hong Kong under British Rule

Hong Kong's colonial legacy under British rule is a pivotal chapter in its history, shaping its identity, governance, and culture in profound ways. The British presence in Hong Kong began in the 19th century following the First Opium War, when the Qing Dynasty ceded Hong Kong Island to Britain under the Treaty of Nanking in 1842. This marked the start of a period of British colonization that would last for over 150 years.

Under British rule, Hong Kong underwent rapid transformation and development. The British implemented various administrative and legal reforms, establishing a system of governance that differed from that of mainland China. British colonial administrators introduced Western-style institutions, including a legal system based on English common law, which laid the groundwork for Hong Kong's future as a global financial center.

One of the most enduring legacies of British rule in Hong Kong is its legal system, which remains based on English common law to this day. This legal framework has played a crucial role in fostering a business-friendly environment and upholding the rule of law, contributing to Hong Kong's reputation as a safe and stable place to do business.

British colonial rule also had a profound impact on Hong Kong's social and cultural landscape. The British brought with them Western customs, traditions, and values, which gradually influenced local society. English became widely spoken and taught in schools, alongside Cantonese and other Chinese dialects, leading to a bilingual and multicultural society.

Economically, British rule propelled Hong Kong into a major center of trade and commerce in the Asia-Pacific region. The city's strategic location, coupled with its efficient port facilities and favorable business environment, attracted investors and entrepreneurs from around the world. Hong Kong became known as the "Gateway to China," serving as a vital conduit for trade between East and West.

Despite the economic prosperity brought about by British rule, there were also challenges and tensions, particularly in the realm of politics. Hong Kong's colonial government was characterized by limited democracy and representation, with power largely concentrated in the hands of British officials and a small elite class of local elites. This led to calls for greater autonomy and democracy, which would become more pronounced in the years leading up to the handover to China in 1997.

Overall, the legacy of British colonial rule in Hong Kong is complex and multifaceted, encompassing both positive and negative aspects. While the British presence brought economic prosperity, modernization, and the rule of law, it also left behind a legacy of political inequality and social divisions. As we delve deeper into Hong Kong's colonial history, we will gain a deeper understanding of the forces that have shaped this unique city into the global metropolis it is today.

Return to China: The Handover and Its Implications

The handover of Hong Kong from British to Chinese sovereignty in 1997 marked a significant turning point in the city's history, as well as in international relations. Under the Sino-British Joint Declaration signed in 1984, Britain agreed to return Hong Kong to China, with the condition that the city would retain a high degree of autonomy under the "one country, two systems" principle. This arrangement was intended to ensure Hong Kong's continued economic prosperity, social stability, and way of life after the handover.

On July 1, 1997, Hong Kong's sovereignty was formally transferred to China in a ceremony attended by dignitaries from both countries, including British Prime Minister Tony Blair and Chinese President Jiang Zemin. The event was marked by celebrations and symbolism, as the British colonial flag was lowered for the last time and replaced by the Chinese national flag.

The handover of Hong Kong to China had significant implications for the city's political, economic, and social landscape. Under the terms of the handover, Hong Kong was designated a Special Administrative Region (SAR) of China, with its own legal system, currency, and government. The Basic Law, a mini-constitution drafted by China, serves as the legal framework governing Hong Kong's autonomy and relationship with the central government in Beijing.

One of the key principles of the "one country, two systems" arrangement is the preservation of Hong Kong's capitalist economy and way of life. Hong Kong retains its status as a global financial hub and international trade center, with its own currency, the Hong Kong dollar, and a free-market economy. The city's legal system, based on English common law, also remains intact, providing a level of judicial independence and protection of individual rights.

However, despite assurances of autonomy, there have been concerns about the erosion of Hong Kong's freedoms and autonomy in recent years. The implementation of controversial national security legislation in 2020 sparked protests and international condemnation, amid fears that it would undermine Hong Kong's civil liberties and rule of law. The crackdown on dissent and pro-democracy activists has raised questions about the future of Hong Kong's autonomy and its relationship with the central government in Beijing.

The handover of Hong Kong to China also had implications for its international relations and geopolitical significance. Hong Kong's status as a global financial center and gateway to China has made it a key player in international trade and diplomacy. Its unique position as a bridge between East and West has given it a strategic importance that extends far beyond its borders.

As we reflect on the handover of Hong Kong to China and its implications, it is clear that the city's future is intertwined with the complex dynamics of Chinese politics, global economics, and regional stability. The legacy of the handover continues to shape Hong Kong's identity and its place in the world, as it navigates the challenges and opportunities of the 21st century.

Governance and Politics: One Country, Two Systems

The governance and politics of Hong Kong under the "one country, two systems" framework are a complex interplay of Chinese sovereignty and Hong Kong's unique autonomy. This arrangement, established after the handover from British to Chinese rule in 1997, was intended to allow Hong Kong to maintain its distinct legal, economic, and political systems while being part of the People's Republic of China.

Under the Basic Law, Hong Kong's mini-constitution, the city enjoys a high degree of autonomy in areas such as trade, finance, and immigration. It has its own legal system based on English common law, separate from the mainland's socialist legal system. Hong Kong also maintains control over its currency, the Hong Kong dollar, and its own government, led by a Chief Executive.

The Chief Executive is the highest-ranking official in Hong Kong and is appointed by a 1,200-member Election Committee, dominated by pro-Beijing elites. While Hong Kong residents have the right to vote for their Chief Executive, the pool of candidates is vetted by Beijing, leading to criticism of limited democratic participation.

The Legislative Council (LegCo) is Hong Kong's legislative body, responsible for making laws and overseeing the government. It consists of 70 members, with some directly elected by the public and others chosen by functional constituencies representing various sectors of society. The composition of LegCo reflects Hong Kong's diverse political landscape, with pro-democracy and pro-Beijing factions vying for influence.

Despite its autonomy, Hong Kong's governance is subject to oversight and intervention from the central government in Beijing. The Basic Law grants Beijing ultimate authority over matters of national security and foreign affairs, and Beijing has the power to interpret and amend the Basic Law as it sees fit.

In recent years, tensions over Hong Kong's political future have escalated, fueled by concerns about the erosion of civil liberties and democratic freedoms. The 2014 Umbrella Movement, sparked by Beijing's decision to restrict electoral reforms, saw widespread protests and civil disobedience, highlighting growing dissatisfaction with the status quo.

The 2019 anti-extradition bill protests, which evolved into a broader pro-democracy movement, further strained relations between Hong Kong and Beijing. The protests, characterized by mass rallies, clashes with police, and international attention, underscored deep-seated grievances over issues such as electoral reform, police brutality, and Beijing's encroachment on Hong Kong's autonomy.

In response to the protests, Beijing imposed a controversial national security law on Hong Kong in 2020, criminalizing acts of secession, subversion, terrorism, and collusion with foreign forces. The law, criticized for its vague and broad provisions, has raised concerns about its impact on Hong Kong's freedoms and rule of law, leading to further tensions and uncertainty about the city's future.

As Hong Kong grapples with the complexities of governance and politics under the "one country, two systems" framework, it faces challenges and opportunities in balancing its autonomy with its relationship with Beijing. The outcome of this delicate balance will shape Hong Kong's future as a global city and its role in the evolving dynamics of China's rise on the world stage.

Economic Powerhouse: Hong Kong as a Financial Hub

Hong Kong's status as a financial powerhouse is a testament to its strategic location, robust infrastructure, and business-friendly environment. As one of the world's leading international financial centers, Hong Kong plays a pivotal role in global finance, trade, and investment.

The city's financial sector is anchored by its stock exchange, the Hong Kong Stock Exchange (HKEX), which ranks among the largest and most active in the world. With a market capitalization exceeding trillions of dollars, the HKEX serves as a primary venue for companies to raise capital through initial public offerings (IPOs) and secondary listings.

Hong Kong's banking sector is also a key pillar of its financial industry, with a strong presence of both local and international banks. The city's banks offer a wide range of financial services, including corporate banking, wealth management, and cross-border financing, catering to the diverse needs of businesses and individuals.

In addition to traditional banking, Hong Kong is a global leader in fintech innovation and digital finance. The city's regulatory environment, coupled with its advanced infrastructure and talent pool, has fostered a thriving ecosystem of fintech startups and companies. From mobile payments and blockchain technology to robo-advisors and peer-to-peer lending platforms, Hong Kong is at the forefront of shaping the future of finance.

Hong Kong's role as a financial hub extends beyond banking and capital markets to include asset management, insurance, and professional services. The city is home to a vibrant community of asset managers, hedge funds, and private equity firms, managing trillions of dollars in assets for clients around the world. Its insurance industry, known for its stability and regulatory oversight, offers a wide range of products and services to businesses and individuals.

The presence of leading international accounting and legal firms further reinforces Hong Kong's position as a global financial center. These firms provide a wide range of professional services, including auditing, tax advisory, and legal counsel, supporting the needs of multinational corporations and financial institutions operating in the region.

Hong Kong's success as a financial hub is also driven by its connectivity and openness to the global economy. The city's strategic location at the crossroads of East and West, coupled with its efficient transportation and communication networks, makes it a preferred destination for businesses and investors looking to access markets in Asia and beyond.

Despite its strengths, Hong Kong faces challenges in maintaining its status as a financial hub in an increasingly competitive and rapidly evolving global landscape. Competition from regional rivals, geopolitical tensions, and regulatory reforms pose risks to the city's competitiveness and attractiveness as a financial center.

As Hong Kong navigates these challenges, its resilience, adaptability, and commitment to innovation will be crucial in ensuring its continued success as a leading international financial hub. By leveraging its strengths and embracing opportunities in emerging sectors such as fintech and green finance, Hong Kong can continue to play a vital role in shaping the future of global finance.

Skyscrapers and Skyline: The Architectural Marvels

Hong Kong's skyline is an awe-inspiring testament to human ingenuity and architectural innovation. As one of the most densely populated cities in the world, Hong Kong's vertical landscape is dominated by towering skyscrapers that reach towards the heavens, creating a stunning visual spectacle that captivates visitors and residents alike.

At the heart of Hong Kong's skyline is Central, the city's bustling financial district, where gleaming skyscrapers soar into the clouds, symbolizing the city's status as a global financial hub. Among the most iconic landmarks is the International Commerce Centre (ICC), a towering skyscraper that stands as the tallest building in Hong Kong, boasting unparalleled views of Victoria Harbour and the surrounding cityscape.

Adjacent to the ICC is the Two International Finance Centre (IFC), another architectural marvel that houses offices, shops, and restaurants, as well as the luxurious Four Seasons Hotel. Its sleek design and striking silhouette make it a distinctive feature of Hong Kong's skyline, visible from miles away.

Not far from Central is the West Kowloon Cultural District, a sprawling waterfront development that is home to a diverse array of cultural venues, including the striking Hong Kong Cultural Centre and the futuristic Xiqu Centre, dedicated to the preservation and promotion of traditional Chinese opera.

Across Victoria Harbour in Kowloon, the skyline is punctuated by landmarks such as the iconic Clock Tower and the historic Tsim Sha Tsui waterfront, where visitors can admire panoramic views of Hong Kong Island's skyline shimmering across the water.

In addition to its modern skyscrapers, Hong Kong's skyline also features a rich tapestry of architectural styles, reflecting its colonial past and multicultural heritage. Historic landmarks such as the Legislative Council Building and the former Central Police Station stand as reminders of Hong Kong's colonial legacy, while traditional Chinese temples and shrines offer glimpses into the city's cultural heritage.

As Hong Kong continues to grow and evolve, its skyline remains a symbol of progress, innovation, and resilience. From towering skyscrapers to historic landmarks, each building tells a story of Hong Kong's past, present, and future, shaping the city's identity as a dynamic and vibrant metropolis at the crossroads of East and West.

Natural Wonders: Exploring Hong Kong's Wildlife and Parks

Hong Kong's natural wonders are a hidden gem waiting to be discovered by those who venture beyond the city's bustling streets. Despite its reputation as a concrete jungle, Hong Kong is home to a diverse range of ecosystems, from lush forests and rugged mountains to pristine beaches and marine parks.

One of the most remarkable natural features of Hong Kong is its extensive network of country parks and nature reserves, which cover approximately 40% of the territory's land area. These protected areas provide sanctuary for a rich array of flora and fauna, including rare and endangered species such as the Chinese white dolphin, the black-faced spoonbill, and the Chinese pangolin.

Among the most popular destinations for nature lovers is the Hong Kong Global Geopark, a UNESCO-listed site renowned for its stunning geological formations and dramatic landscapes. Visitors can explore ancient rock formations, sea caves, and volcanic landscapes, offering a glimpse into Hong Kong's geological history dating back millions of years.

For those seeking adventure, Hong Kong offers a wealth of hiking trails that wind through its rugged terrain, offering panoramic views of the city skyline, lush valleys, and sparkling coastlines. The Dragon's

Back Trail, named one of the world's best urban hikes by National Geographic, offers stunning vistas of Shek O Beach and the South China Sea, while the MacLehose Trail traverses the scenic landscapes of the New Territories.

In addition to its terrestrial wonders, Hong Kong boasts a vibrant marine ecosystem teeming with life. The city's waters are home to a diverse array of marine species, including coral reefs, seagrass beds, and mangrove forests. The Hong Kong Marine Park, located in the pristine waters of Sai Kung, is a haven for marine biodiversity, offering opportunities for snorkeling, diving, and eco-tours.

Hong Kong's natural wonders are not limited to its parks and reserves; its urban green spaces also provide refuge from the hustle and bustle of city life. The Hong Kong Zoological and Botanical Gardens, located in the heart of Central, is home to a diverse collection of plants and animals, including rare orchids, giant pandas, and flamingos.

As Hong Kong continues to develop and urbanize, the conservation of its natural wonders becomes increasingly important. Efforts to preserve and protect Hong Kong's biodiversity are underway, including habitat restoration projects, species conservation initiatives, and sustainable ecotourism practices. By embracing its natural heritage, Hong Kong can ensure that future generations will continue to enjoy and appreciate the beauty and diversity of its wildlife and parks.

From Dim Sum to Michelin Stars: A Culinary Journey

Embark on a culinary journey through the vibrant and diverse flavors of Hong Kong, where every bite tells a story of tradition, innovation, and culinary excellence. From humble street stalls to Michelin-starred restaurants, Hong Kong offers a tantalizing array of culinary delights that reflect its rich cultural heritage and cosmopolitan character.

At the heart of Hong Kong's culinary scene is dim sum, a beloved tradition that has been passed down through generations. These bite-sized delicacies, ranging from steamed dumplings and buns to savory pastries and desserts, are enjoyed by locals and visitors alike in bustling teahouses and dim sum parlors across the city. Popular dim sum dishes include har gow (shrimp dumplings), siu mai (pork dumplings), and char siu bao (barbecue pork buns), each crafted with meticulous care and attention to detail.

Beyond dim sum, Hong Kong boasts a diverse range of regional Chinese cuisines, reflecting the city's multicultural population and historical ties to mainland China. Cantonese cuisine, with its emphasis on fresh ingredients and delicate flavors, reigns supreme in Hong Kong, offering a tantalizing array of seafood, soups, and stir-fries. Savor the flavors of classic Cantonese dishes such as roast duck, crispy pork belly, and steamed fish with ginger and scallions, prepared with skill and precision by master chefs.

In recent years, Hong Kong has emerged as a culinary destination for gourmet dining, with a growing number of Michelin-starred restaurants earning international acclaim. From innovative fusion cuisine to traditional Chinese specialties with a modern twist, Hong Kong's Michelin-starred restaurants offer an unparalleled dining experience that tantalizes the taste buds and delights the senses. Indulge in exquisite tasting menus, paired with fine wines and impeccable service, as you savor the finest flavors from around the world.

For those seeking a taste of Hong Kong's street food scene, look no further than the city's vibrant night markets and food stalls, where aromatic aromas and sizzling sounds fill the air. Sample local favorites such as curry fish balls, egg waffles, and stinky tofu, washed down with a refreshing glass of sugar cane juice or herbal tea. These affordable and delicious snacks offer a glimpse into the everyday culinary delights enjoyed by Hong Kongers.

No culinary journey through Hong Kong would be complete without exploring its vibrant seafood scene. With its proximity to the South China Sea, Hong Kong boasts an abundance of fresh seafood, from succulent lobster and crab to plump oysters and clams. Visit bustling seafood markets such as Sai Kung or Lei Yue Mun, where you can handpick your seafood and have it cooked to perfection by local chefs.

As you savor the flavors of Hong Kong, you'll discover that food is more than just sustenance; it's a celebration of culture, community, and creativity. Whether you're dining at a Michelin-starred restaurant or enjoying a humble bowl of noodles from a street vendor, each culinary experience offers a glimpse into the rich tapestry of flavors that make Hong Kong a gastronomic paradise.

Tea Culture: Tradition in Every Sip

Tea culture runs deep in the veins of Hong Kong, weaving its way through the fabric of daily life with a reverence that transcends mere beverage consumption. From traditional tea ceremonies to casual gatherings over a cup of milk tea, tea holds a special place in the hearts of Hong Kongers, symbolizing hospitality, community, and tradition.

One of the most iconic teas in Hong Kong is the humble milk tea, known locally as "lai cha" or "nai cha." This creamy and aromatic concoction, made from a blend of strong black tea and evaporated or condensed milk, has become synonymous with Hong Kong's culinary identity. Whether enjoyed in a bustling cha chaan teng (tea restaurant) or served on a street corner from a dai pai dong (open-air food stall), milk tea is a beloved beverage that brings people together, regardless of social class or background.

Beyond milk tea, Hong Kong boasts a rich variety of teas, ranging from delicate green teas to robust pu'erh teas, each with its own unique flavor profile and health benefits. Traditional Chinese tea ceremonies, rooted in centuries-old rituals and customs, offer a meditative and contemplative experience that honors the artistry and craftsmanship of tea making. Tea connoisseurs can explore the nuances of different tea varieties, from the floral notes of jasmine tea to the earthy richness of oolong tea, through guided tastings and workshops held at tea houses and specialty shops throughout the city.

just browsing for souvenirs, Cat Street offers a fascinating glimpse into Hong Kong's rich cultural heritage.

For a taste of local flavor and community spirit, visit one of Hong Kong's many wet markets, where locals shop for fresh produce, seafood, and meat. These lively markets are a feast for the senses, with colorful displays of fruits and vegetables, the aroma of spices and herbs, and the hustle and bustle of vendors and shoppers alike. Experience the vibrant atmosphere of markets such as the Graham Street Market or the Tai Po Market, where you can immerse yourself in the sights, sounds, and smells of everyday life in Hong Kong.

For a more upscale shopping experience, head to one of Hong Kong's luxury malls or designer boutiques, where you'll find an array of high-end fashion brands, gourmet dining options, and world-class entertainment. From the iconic shopping districts of Causeway Bay and Tsim Sha Tsui to the glitzy malls of Central and Admiralty, Hong Kong offers a wealth of retail therapy for even the most discerning shopper.

Whether you're hunting for bargains at a bustling street market or indulging in luxury shopping at a high-end mall, Hong Kong's markets offer something for everyone. With their vibrant atmosphere, diverse offerings, and unique cultural experiences, these must-visit markets are an essential part of any trip to this dynamic city.

Iconic Landmarks: Exploring Hong Kong's Tourist Sights

Exploring Hong Kong's tourist sights is like embarking on a journey through history, culture, and modernity all at once. The city's iconic landmarks offer a kaleidoscope of experiences that captivate visitors from around the world.

At the top of any tourist's must-visit list is Victoria Peak, the highest point on Hong Kong Island and home to some of the most breathtaking views of the city skyline. Take a ride on the historic Peak Tram to reach the summit, where you can admire panoramic vistas of Victoria Harbour, towering skyscrapers, and lush mountainsides stretching as far as the eye can see.

No visit to Hong Kong is complete without a trip to the Big Buddha, one of the largest outdoor seated bronze Buddhas in the world. Located on Lantau Island, this majestic statue stands at over 34 meters tall and is a symbol of peace, harmony, and enlightenment. Visitors can climb the 268 steps to reach the base of the statue and explore the surrounding Po Lin Monastery and Ngong Ping Village.

For a taste of Hong Kong's colonial past, head to the historic neighborhood of Central and visit landmarks such as the iconic Clock Tower and the historic Former Police Headquarters, which now houses the Tai Kwun Centre for Heritage and Arts. Take a stroll along the picturesque waterfront promenade of Tsim Sha Tsui and admire the stunning views of Victoria Harbour, framed by the towering skyline of Hong Kong Island.

Step back in time and immerse yourself in the rich cultural heritage of Hong Kong at the Man Mo Temple, a historic Taoist temple dedicated to the gods of literature and war. Marvel at the intricate wood carvings, ornate incense coils, and serene atmosphere of this centuries-old sanctuary, tucked away amidst the hustle and bustle of the city.

For a taste of Hong Kong's modernity and innovation, visit the West Kowloon Cultural District, a dynamic waterfront precinct that is home to world-class cultural venues such as the Hong Kong Cultural Centre, the M+ Museum of Visual Culture, and the Xiqu Centre for Chinese opera. Take a leisurely stroll along the Avenue of Stars and admire the stunning views of the city skyline, or catch a performance at the iconic Hong Kong Space Museum.

From ancient temples and historic landmarks to cutting-edge cultural institutions and panoramic vistas, exploring Hong Kong's tourist sights is a journey of discovery that offers something for everyone. Whether you're a history buff, culture vulture, or avid photographer, these iconic landmarks are sure to leave a lasting impression and create memories that will last a lifetime.

Hong Kong Disneyland: Where Magic Meets the East

Hong Kong Disneyland is a magical destination that enchants visitors of all ages with its blend of Disney charm and Asian influences. Located on Lantau Island, this world-class theme park is a beloved attraction that offers a unique twist on the classic Disney experience.

Opened in 2005, Hong Kong Disneyland is the first Disney theme park to be built in China and the second in Asia, after Tokyo Disneyland. Spanning over 300 acres, the park is divided into several themed lands, each offering its own immersive attractions, entertainment, and dining experiences.

Main Street, U.S.A. welcomes guests with its charming turn-of-the-century architecture and nostalgic atmosphere, reminiscent of small-town America. Here, visitors can stroll down quaint streets lined with shops, eateries, and entertainment venues, or catch a glimpse of the daily parade featuring beloved Disney characters.

Adventureland beckons adventurers to embark on thrilling expeditions through exotic jungles, ancient ruins, and swashbuckling pirate encounters. Highlights include the iconic Jungle River Cruise, where guests board safari boats to explore mysterious waterways teeming with animatronic wildlife, and the exhilarating Big Grizzly Mountain Runaway Mine Cars roller coaster.

Fantasyland is a realm of enchantment and wonder, where fairy tales come to life in vibrant, immersive attractions inspired by classic Disney films. From soaring high above the clouds with Dumbo the Flying Elephant to journeying through the whimsical world of "it's a small world," there's no shortage of magical experiences to be had in this charming land.

Tomorrowland offers a glimpse into the future with its sleek, futuristic architecture and high-tech attractions. Blast off into space aboard the thrilling Hyperspace Mountain roller coaster, soar through the skies on the Orbitron, or embark on an intergalactic adventure with Buzz Lightyear on Buzz Lightyear Astro Blasters.

For a taste of Chinese culture and tradition, guests can explore the unique offerings of Mystic Point and Toy Story Land. Mystic Point invites visitors to uncover the mysteries of Lord Henry Mystic's Manor, a haunted house filled with enchanted artifacts and supernatural surprises, while Toy Story Land immerses guests in the playful world of Woody, Buzz, and the gang, with larger-than-life attractions and whimsical scenery.

In addition to its themed lands and attractions, Hong Kong Disneyland offers a wide range of entertainment options, including live shows, parades, character meet-and-greets, and seasonal events. From dazzling fireworks displays to festive celebrations during Chinese New Year, there's always something magical happening at the Happiest Place on Earth.

With its blend of Disney magic and Eastern charm, Hong Kong Disneyland is a truly enchanting destination that delights and entertains visitors from near and far. Whether you're a lifelong Disney fan or a first-time visitor, this magical theme park promises an unforgettable experience filled with laughter, adventure, and cherished memories that will last a lifetime.

Lantau Island: Nature, Spirituality, and the Big Buddha

Lantau Island, the largest island in Hong Kong, is a haven of natural beauty, spirituality, and cultural heritage. Located just a short ferry ride away from the bustling city center, Lantau offers visitors a tranquil escape from the urban hustle and bustle, with its pristine beaches, lush mountains, and serene villages.

One of the island's most iconic landmarks is the Tian Tan Buddha, also known as the Big Buddha, a majestic statue that stands at over 34 meters tall and weighs more than 250 metric tons. Perched atop Ngong Ping Plateau, the Big Buddha is a symbol of harmony, enlightenment, and compassion, overlooking the scenic landscape of Lantau Island and offering breathtaking views of the surrounding mountains and sea.

To reach the Big Buddha, visitors can embark on a journey along the Ngong Ping 360 cable car, which takes passengers on a scenic ride across the island's verdant valleys and rolling hills. The cable car journey offers panoramic views of Lantau's stunning natural landscapes, including the lush greenery of Lantau Country Park and the tranquil waters of Tung Chung Bay.

Upon arriving at Ngong Ping Village, visitors can explore the cultural attractions and spiritual sites that surround the Big Buddha, including the Po Lin

Monastery, a Buddhist monastery that dates back to the early 20th century. Marvel at the monastery's ornate architecture, tranquil gardens, and intricate wood carvings, or join the monks in meditation and prayer as they go about their daily rituals.

For those seeking adventure, Lantau Island offers a wealth of outdoor activities and recreational opportunities, from hiking and mountain biking to camping and birdwatching. The island is home to several scenic hiking trails, including the Lantau Trail, a 70-kilometer route that winds its way through lush forests, secluded beaches, and picturesque villages, offering stunning views of the island's natural beauty along the way.

Lantau's coastal areas are also popular destinations for water sports enthusiasts, with opportunities for swimming, kayaking, and windsurfing at beaches such as Cheung Sha Beach and Pui O Beach. Nature lovers can explore the island's diverse ecosystems, including wetlands, mangrove forests, and coral reefs, which are home to a rich variety of plant and animal species, including migratory birds, butterflies, and marine life.

In addition to its natural attractions, Lantau Island is also steeped in history and culture, with ancient fishing villages, historic temples, and traditional festivals that celebrate the island's heritage. Whether you're seeking spiritual enlightenment, outdoor adventure, or cultural immersion, Lantau Island offers a truly immersive experience that captivates the senses and nourishes the soul.

Kowloon: A Fusion of Old and New

Kowloon, the vibrant urban district located on the northern side of Hong Kong's Victoria Harbour, is a dynamic blend of old-world charm and modern innovation. From its bustling streets and markets to its towering skyscrapers and cultural landmarks, Kowloon offers visitors a captivating glimpse into the rich tapestry of Hong Kong's past, present, and future.

At the heart of Kowloon lies Tsim Sha Tsui, a bustling neighborhood known for its shopping, dining, and entertainment options. Here, visitors can explore iconic attractions such as the Avenue of Stars, a waterfront promenade that pays tribute to Hong Kong's rich cinematic heritage, and the historic Clock Tower, a remnant of the city's colonial past. Tsim Sha Tsui is also home to a vibrant arts and culture scene, with galleries, theaters, and performance venues showcasing local and international talent.

Adjacent to Tsim Sha Tsui is Mong Kok, a lively district known for its bustling markets, vibrant street scenes, and eclectic mix of shops and eateries. Here, visitors can immerse themselves in the sensory overload of the Mong Kok Ladies' Market, where vendors sell everything from clothing and accessories to electronics and souvenirs. Nearby, the Temple Street Night Market comes alive after sunset, offering a lively atmosphere and a wide selection of street food, fortune tellers, and bargain finds.

For a taste of Kowloon's rich cultural heritage, visitors can explore historic landmarks such as the Wong Tai Sin Temple, a Taoist temple dedicated to the god of healing and fortune. Marvel at the temple's colorful architecture, intricate decorations, and tranquil gardens, or join the locals in prayer and offerings as they seek blessings for health, prosperity, and good fortune.

For those seeking a taste of Kowloon's modern side, the district offers a wealth of shopping, dining, and entertainment options, from luxury malls and designer boutiques to trendy cafes and rooftop bars. Explore the upscale boutiques of Elements Mall in West Kowloon, or indulge in gourmet dining at one of the district's many Michelin-starred restaurants. After dark, experience the vibrant nightlife of Kowloon's entertainment districts, where live music venues, nightclubs, and rooftop bars offer endless opportunities for fun and excitement.

Throughout Kowloon, visitors will encounter a dynamic blend of old and new, where ancient temples and historic landmarks stand side by side with sleek skyscrapers and modern amenities. Whether you're exploring the bustling streets of Mong Kok or admiring the stunning views of Victoria Harbour from Tsim Sha Tsui, Kowloon offers a fascinating glimpse into the diverse and dynamic spirit of Hong Kong.

The New Territories: Exploring Hong Kong's Countryside

The New Territories of Hong Kong offer a captivating contrast to the bustling urban landscape of the city, with its tranquil countryside, picturesque villages, and lush greenery stretching as far as the eye can see. As the largest region in Hong Kong, the New Territories encompass a diverse array of landscapes, from rugged mountains and rolling hills to fertile farmland and pristine coastline.

One of the highlights of the New Territories is its extensive network of hiking trails, which wind their way through scenic countryside, offering breathtaking views of mountains, valleys, and coastline. Popular hiking destinations include the Sai Kung East Country Park, where visitors can explore rugged coastlines, secluded beaches, and pristine islands accessible only by boat or foot. The MacLehose Trail, a 100-kilometer-long trail that traverses the New Territories, offers hikers the opportunity to experience the region's diverse landscapes and natural beauty.

For those interested in cultural heritage, the New Territories is home to a wealth of historic villages, temples, and monuments that offer a glimpse into Hong Kong's rich history and heritage. Visit the walled village of Kat Hing Wai, one of the best-preserved walled villages in Hong Kong, where traditional Hakka architecture and customs have been preserved for centuries. Explore the ancient walled village of Tsang Tai Uk, a fortified Hakka village dating back to the 19th century, or visit the historic Tai Fu Tai Mansion, a stately home built in the Qing dynasty style.

The New Territories is also home to several important ecological sites, including the Mai Po Marshes Nature Reserve, a haven for migratory birds and wetland wildlife. Birdwatchers can spot a wide variety of bird species, including egrets, herons, and migratory waterfowl, while nature lovers can explore the reserve's diverse habitats, including mudflats, mangroves, and freshwater ponds.

For those seeking a taste of rural life, the New Territories offers opportunities to experience traditional farming practices and village life. Visit the Kam Tin Walled Village, where you can learn about traditional farming methods and sample local produce at the farmers' market, or take a leisurely bike ride through the scenic countryside, stopping to explore charming villages and picturesque landscapes along the way.

Whether you're seeking outdoor adventure, cultural immersion, or simply a peaceful retreat from the hustle and bustle of city life, the New Territories of Hong Kong offers something for everyone. With its diverse landscapes, rich cultural heritage, and abundance of outdoor activities, the New Territories invites visitors to explore, discover, and reconnect with nature and tradition in this scenic and tranquil corner of Hong Kong.

Macau: The Vegas of the East

Macau, often referred to as the "Vegas of the East," is a vibrant and dynamic city that captivates visitors with its glittering skyline, world-class entertainment, and rich cultural heritage. Located just a short ferry ride from Hong Kong, Macau is a Special Administrative Region of China known for its bustling casinos, luxury resorts, and historic landmarks.

At the heart of Macau's entertainment scene is the Cotai Strip, a stretch of reclaimed land that is home to some of the world's most extravagant resorts and casinos. Here, visitors can try their luck at iconic gaming destinations such as the Venetian Macao, the largest casino in the world, which boasts an impressive array of gaming tables, slot machines, and entertainment options. Other notable casinos on the Cotai Strip include the City of Dreams, the Wynn Macau, and the MGM Grand Macau, each offering a unique blend of gaming, dining, and entertainment experiences.

Beyond its casinos, Macau is also renowned for its rich cultural heritage and historic landmarks. The Historic Centre of Macau, a UNESCO World Heritage Site, is home to a wealth of well-preserved colonial buildings, ancient temples, and historic squares that reflect the city's unique blend of East and West. Visitors can explore landmarks such as the Ruins of St. Paul's, a 17th-century Jesuit church facade that is one of Macau's most iconic symbols, and the A-Ma Temple, a Taoist temple dedicated to the goddess of the sea.

For those seeking a taste of Macau's culinary delights, the city offers a diverse array of dining options that showcase its multicultural heritage. Macanese cuisine, a fusion of Chinese and Portuguese flavors, is a highlight of the city's culinary scene, with dishes such as Portuguese egg tarts, African chicken, and bacalhau (salted cod) featuring prominently on menus across the city. Visitors can also sample traditional Chinese and international cuisine at a variety of restaurants, street food stalls, and food markets scattered throughout the city.

In addition to its casinos, cultural landmarks, and culinary delights, Macau also offers a wide range of shopping, entertainment, and recreational activities for visitors to enjoy. Explore the bustling streets of Senado Square, Macau's historic city center, where you'll find charming shops, cafes, and colonial-era architecture. Catch a performance at the Macau Cultural Centre or the Macau Tower, which offers stunning views of the city skyline from its observation deck. And don't forget to take a leisurely stroll along the waterfront promenade of Nam Van Lake, where you can admire the city's skyline illuminated against the night sky.

With its blend of gaming excitement, cultural heritage, and cosmopolitan charm, Macau truly lives up to its reputation as the "Vegas of the East." Whether you're drawn to its glitzy casinos, historic landmarks, or vibrant cultural scene, Macau offers a unique and unforgettable experience that captures the spirit of East-meets-West in the heart of Asia.

Colonial Charm: Historic Buildings and Neighborhoods

Colonial charm infuses Hong Kong's landscape, weaving through historic buildings and neighborhoods that stand as tangible reminders of its colonial past. From elegant colonial-era architecture to quaint streets lined with pastel-hued buildings, these remnants of British rule offer a glimpse into Hong Kong's rich history and cultural heritage.

One of the most iconic examples of colonial architecture in Hong Kong is the former Legislative Council Building, located in Central. Built in 1912, this grand neoclassical building served as the seat of government during the colonial era and is now a declared monument, preserved as a symbol of Hong Kong's democratic heritage. Nearby, the former Central Police Station Compound, now known as Tai Kwun, has been transformed into a vibrant cultural complex, with museums, galleries, and performance spaces housed within its historic walls.

In the heart of Kowloon, the Peninsula Hotel stands as a timeless symbol of colonial elegance and luxury. Built in 1928, this iconic hotel has played host to royalty, dignitaries, and celebrities over the years and remains one of Hong Kong's most prestigious landmarks. Its elegant colonial-era facade and opulent interiors evoke a sense of old-world glamour and sophistication that continues to enchant guests to this day.

Elsewhere in Kowloon, the charming neighborhood of Kowloon City boasts a wealth of colonial-era architecture, including the historic Kowloon Walled City Park. Once a lawless enclave known for its overcrowded tenements and illicit activities, the walled city was demolished in the 1990s and transformed into a peaceful park that preserves the remnants of its storied past. Visitors can explore the park's tranquil gardens, ancient walls, and historic artifacts, which offer a fascinating glimpse into the area's tumultuous history.

In the Western District of Hong Kong Island, the neighborhood of Sheung Wan is home to a treasure trove of colonial-era buildings and landmarks. The Western Market, a striking red-brick structure built in 1906, is one of the city's oldest surviving market buildings and is now a designated historic building housing shops and restaurants. Nearby, the Man Mo Temple, a historic Taoist temple dating back to the mid-19th century, is another architectural gem that reflects Hong Kong's multicultural heritage.

Throughout Hong Kong, colonial-era buildings and neighborhoods serve as living testaments to the city's past, preserving its rich architectural heritage for future generations to enjoy and appreciate. Whether exploring the elegant streets of Central, the bustling markets of Kowloon, or the tranquil parks of Sheung Wan, visitors can immerse themselves in the colonial charm of Hong Kong and experience firsthand the enduring legacy of its colonial history.

Victoria Harbour: The Heartbeat of Hong Kong

Victoria Harbour, the iconic body of water that separates Hong Kong Island from the Kowloon Peninsula, is undeniably the heartbeat of Hong Kong. With its stunning skyline, bustling port, and vibrant waterfront promenades, Victoria Harbour is not only a vital transportation hub but also a symbol of the city's dynamism, energy, and resilience.

Stretching for approximately three kilometers from east to west, Victoria Harbour serves as a natural harbor for Hong Kong's bustling port, one of the busiest in the world. Every day, thousands of ships, ferries, and boats navigate the harbor's waters, transporting goods, passengers, and cargo to and from destinations around the globe. From massive container ships to traditional Chinese junks, the harbor is a hive of activity, with vessels of all shapes and sizes crisscrossing its waters day and night.

But Victoria Harbour is more than just a busy port; it's also a scenic and recreational destination that attracts millions of visitors each year. The harbor's waterfront promenades, such as the Tsim Sha Tsui Promenade and the Central Waterfront Promenade, offer stunning views of the city skyline, with towering skyscrapers, glittering lights, and iconic landmarks such as the Bank of China Tower and the International Commerce Centre.

One of the best ways to experience Victoria Harbour is by taking a leisurely cruise on one of the city's famous Star Ferry boats. Operating since 1888, the Star Ferry offers affordable and scenic transportation across the harbor, with routes connecting Central on Hong Kong Island with Tsim Sha Tsui and Wan Chai on the Kowloon Peninsula. The short journey provides passengers with panoramic views of the harbor and skyline, making it a favorite activity for both tourists and locals alike.

In addition to ferry rides, visitors can also enjoy a variety of leisure activities along the harborfront, including jogging, cycling, and picnicking in one of the many waterfront parks and gardens. At night, the harbor comes alive with dazzling light shows and fireworks displays, such as the Symphony of Lights, a multimedia spectacle that illuminates the city skyline with synchronized music and laser beams.

Victoria Harbour is not only a vital economic lifeline and transportation artery but also a symbol of Hong Kong's spirit and identity. Its bustling waters, iconic skyline, and scenic waterfront promenades embody the energy, diversity, and vitality of this dynamic city, making it truly the heartbeat of Hong Kong.

Avenue of Stars: Honoring Hong Kong's Film Industry

The Avenue of Stars, located along the Tsim Sha Tsui waterfront in Hong Kong, is a tribute to the city's vibrant film industry and the stars who have contributed to its success. Modeled after the Hollywood Walk of Fame, the Avenue of Stars features plaques, handprints, and statues honoring some of Hong Kong's most beloved actors, directors, and other industry professionals.

Opened in 2004, the Avenue of Stars quickly became a popular tourist attraction, offering visitors a chance to walk in the footsteps of their favorite movie stars and learn about the history and impact of Hong Kong cinema. The promenade stretches for about 440 meters along the waterfront, providing stunning views of Victoria Harbour and the city skyline as a backdrop to the star-studded walkway.

One of the most iconic features of the Avenue of Stars is the bronze statue of Bruce Lee, the legendary martial artist and actor who is widely regarded as one of Hong Kong's most iconic cultural figures. Standing at over two meters tall, the statue depicts Lee in a dynamic martial arts pose, paying homage to his influence on the global film industry and popular culture.

In addition to the Bruce Lee statue, the Avenue of Stars is also home to statues and memorials honoring other luminaries of Hong Kong cinema, including actors such as Jackie Chan, Chow Yun-fat, and Andy

Lau, as well as directors such as John Woo and Tsui Hark. Visitors can stroll along the promenade and admire these tributes to the stars who have made significant contributions to the city's film industry.

Throughout the Avenue of Stars, visitors will also find information panels and displays that provide insight into the history and evolution of Hong Kong cinema, from its humble beginnings in the early 20th century to its rise as a global powerhouse in the 1980s and beyond. Exhibits showcase iconic film posters, artifacts, and memorabilia, offering a glimpse into the creativity, talent, and innovation that have defined Hong Kong cinema over the years.

In addition to its cultural significance, the Avenue of Stars also serves as a scenic and recreational destination for locals and visitors alike. The promenade is lined with benches, landscaped gardens, and public art installations, providing a peaceful and picturesque setting for leisurely strolls, picnics, and photography sessions against the backdrop of Victoria Harbour.

Overall, the Avenue of Stars is a fitting tribute to the legacy and impact of Hong Kong's film industry, celebrating the stars who have entertained and inspired audiences around the world while showcasing the city's unique cultural heritage and creativity. Whether you're a film buff, a martial arts fan, or simply a visitor looking to experience the magic of Hong Kong cinema, the Avenue of Stars offers a captivating and unforgettable experience that honors the past, present, and future of the silver screen.

Festivals and Celebrations: Colorful Traditions

Festivals and celebrations in Hong Kong are vibrant expressions of the city's rich cultural heritage and diverse community. Throughout the year, residents and visitors alike come together to celebrate a wide range of traditional and modern festivals, each offering a unique blend of rituals, performances, and festivities that reflect Hong Kong's multicultural identity.

One of the most iconic festivals in Hong Kong is the Chinese New Year, also known as the Spring Festival, which marks the beginning of the lunar new year according to the Chinese calendar. Celebrated with colorful parades, dragon and lion dances, and elaborate fireworks displays, Chinese New Year is a time for family reunions, feasting, and cultural traditions. The city comes alive with festive decorations, including red lanterns, paper cuttings, and decorative displays symbolizing prosperity, good fortune, and happiness.

Another highlight of Hong Kong's festival calendar is the Mid-Autumn Festival, also known as the Mooncake Festival, which takes place on the 15th day of the eighth lunar month. This harvest festival is celebrated with lantern displays, moon-gazing gatherings, and the consumption of mooncakes, a traditional pastry filled with sweet or savory fillings. Families come together to enjoy mooncakes and tea while admiring the full moon, which is believed to be at its brightest and fullest on this auspicious night.

For those interested in cultural heritage, the Cheung Chau Bun Festival offers a unique glimpse into traditional Chinese folklore and customs. Held annually on the island of Cheung Chau, the festival features colorful parades, bun towers, and Taoist rituals that date back over a century. The highlight of the festival is the bun scrambling competition, in which participants climb a tower covered with imitation buns to retrieve as many buns as possible, symbolizing good luck and prosperity.

In addition to traditional Chinese festivals, Hong Kong also celebrates a variety of cultural and religious holidays, including Christmas, Easter, and Ramadan, reflecting the city's multicultural population and cosmopolitan character. Each festival is marked by its own unique customs, traditions, and celebrations, offering residents and visitors alike the opportunity to experience the diversity and richness of Hong Kong's cultural tapestry.

Throughout the year, festivals and celebrations in Hong Kong serve as important occasions for community bonding, cultural exchange, and spiritual reflection. Whether you're marveling at the vibrant displays of Chinese New Year, sampling mooncakes during the Mid-Autumn Festival, or participating in the bun scrambling competition at the Cheung Chau Bun Festival, these colorful traditions offer a window into the heart and soul of Hong Kong's cultural identity.

The Art Scene: Creativity in Every Corner

In the vibrant city of Hong Kong, creativity thrives in every corner, making the art scene a dynamic and integral part of its cultural landscape. From contemporary galleries and street art to traditional Chinese arts and cultural institutions, Hong Kong offers a diverse and eclectic mix of artistic expressions that captivate and inspire.

One of the focal points of the art scene in Hong Kong is the burgeoning contemporary art scene, which has gained international recognition in recent years. The city is home to a growing number of contemporary art galleries, such as the Hong Kong Arts Centre, the Asia Society Hong Kong Center, and the Para Site, which showcase the work of both local and international artists across a wide range of mediums and styles. The annual Art Basel Hong Kong, one of the world's premier art fairs, attracts collectors, curators, and art enthusiasts from around the globe, further cementing the city's reputation as a hub for contemporary art.

In addition to contemporary art, Hong Kong also boasts a rich tradition of traditional Chinese arts and crafts, including calligraphy, painting, ceramics, and sculpture. Visitors can explore traditional art forms at cultural institutions such as the Hong Kong Museum of Art, which houses a diverse collection of Chinese art spanning thousands of years. The Chi Lin Nunnery and Nan Lian Garden in Kowloon offer tranquil settings for contemplation and appreciation of traditional Chinese architecture and landscaping.

Street art has also emerged as a vibrant and dynamic aspect of Hong Kong's art scene, with neighborhoods such as Sheung Wan and Central becoming open-air galleries showcasing the work of local and international street artists. From colorful murals and graffiti to interactive installations and urban interventions, street art adds a sense of spontaneity and creativity to the city's urban landscape, inviting passersby to engage with art in unexpected ways.

Cultural institutions play a vital role in nurturing and promoting the arts in Hong Kong, with venues such as the Hong Kong Cultural Centre, the Tai Kwun Centre for Heritage and Arts, and the Hong Kong Fringe Club offering a diverse array of performances, exhibitions, and cultural events throughout the year. From classical music concerts and ballet performances to experimental theater and multimedia installations, these venues provide platforms for artists and performers to showcase their talents and engage with audiences from all walks of life.

Overall, the art scene in Hong Kong is a dynamic and ever-evolving tapestry of creativity, innovation, and cultural exchange. Whether you're exploring contemporary galleries, admiring traditional Chinese art, or discovering street art in hidden alleyways, Hong Kong offers endless opportunities to immerse yourself in the vibrant and eclectic world of art and culture.

Mahjong and Tai Chi: Traditional Pastimes

In the bustling streets and tranquil parks of Hong Kong, traditional pastimes such as mahjong and tai chi are deeply ingrained in the fabric of daily life, serving as beloved rituals that connect generations and foster community bonds.

Mahjong, a tile-based game that originated in China during the Qing dynasty, is a popular pastime in Hong Kong and is enjoyed by people of all ages. Played with a set of 144 tiles adorned with Chinese characters and symbols, mahjong is a game of skill, strategy, and luck that requires players to form combinations of tiles in order to win. Whether played in homes, community centers, or outdoor parks, mahjong is a social activity that brings friends and family together for hours of friendly competition and camaraderie.

Tai chi, a traditional Chinese martial art practiced for its health benefits and meditative qualities, is another cherished pastime in Hong Kong. Originating in ancient China, tai chi is characterized by slow, deliberate movements that promote relaxation, balance, and inner harmony. Practiced in parks, gardens, and open spaces throughout the city, tai chi is a daily ritual for many Hong Kong residents, who gather in the early morning hours to perform the graceful movements and breathing exercises that are believed to promote physical and mental well-being.

Both mahjong and tai chi serve as cultural touchstones that reflect the values and traditions of Chinese society, including the importance of family, community, and harmony. In addition to providing entertainment and exercise, these traditional pastimes also offer opportunities for social interaction, cultural exchange, and intergenerational bonding. Whether playing mahjong with friends at a local teahouse or practicing tai chi in the park with a group of strangers, participants in these activities find a sense of connection and belonging that transcends language, age, and background.

In recent years, efforts have been made to preserve and promote these traditional pastimes in Hong Kong, with initiatives aimed at teaching mahjong and tai chi to younger generations and raising awareness of their cultural significance. Mahjong clubs and tai chi associations offer classes, workshops, and events for people of all ages and skill levels, ensuring that these cherished traditions continue to thrive and evolve in the modern world.

In a city known for its fast-paced lifestyle and bustling energy, mahjong and tai chi serve as anchors of tradition and tranquility, providing moments of respite and reflection amidst the chaos of urban life. Whether you're a seasoned mahjong player or a novice tai chi practitioner, these traditional pastimes offer a window into the rich cultural heritage of Hong Kong and provide a sense of continuity and connection in an ever-changing world.

Cantonese Opera: A Theatrical Heritage

Cantonese opera, with its colorful costumes, elaborate makeup, and intricate music, is a cherished theatrical tradition that has been entertaining audiences in Hong Kong and beyond for centuries. Rooted in the cultural heritage of the Guangdong region of China, Cantonese opera combines elements of music, drama, dance, and acrobatics to create a unique and captivating art form that continues to thrive in the modern era.

Dating back to the Tang dynasty (618-907 AD), Cantonese opera evolved from a combination of folk songs, storytelling, and religious rituals that were performed at local festivals and celebrations. Over time, it developed into a sophisticated art form with its own distinct style, repertoire, and performance techniques, influenced by various regional and cultural influences, including Chinese poetry, literature, and martial arts.

Cantonese opera is characterized by its highly stylized performances, which feature a combination of singing, speech, and movement that is steeped in symbolism and tradition. Performers, known as actors, undergo rigorous training from a young age to master the complex vocal techniques, gestures, and facial expressions that are essential to the art form. Each actor specializes in a specific role type, such as sheng (male), dan (female), jing (painted face), or mo (comic), and may spend years perfecting their craft before performing on stage.

The repertoire of Cantonese opera includes a wide range of stories and themes, including historical dramas, mythological legends, and romantic tales, which are often adapted from classic Chinese literature and folklore. These stories are brought to life through a combination of spoken dialogue, sung lyrics, and stylized movements, accompanied by a traditional orchestra consisting of instruments such as drums, gongs, cymbals, and bamboo flutes.

One of the most striking aspects of Cantonese opera is its elaborate costumes and makeup, which play a crucial role in defining characters and conveying emotions on stage. Actors wear intricate costumes adorned with vibrant colors, ornate embroidery, and symbolic motifs that reflect the personality and status of their characters. Makeup, applied with painstaking precision, transforms actors into mythical beings, historical figures, or supernatural creatures, with painted faces and exaggerated features that enhance their dramatic impact.

Despite facing challenges from modern forms of entertainment and changing audience tastes, Cantonese opera remains a beloved cultural institution in Hong Kong, with dedicated theaters, troupes, and festivals dedicated to its preservation and promotion. Organizations such as the Hong Kong Cantonese Opera Troupe and the Chinese Artists Association of Hong Kong work tirelessly to train the next generation of performers and to introduce Cantonese opera to new audiences through educational programs, workshops, and performances.

In recent years, efforts have been made to revitalize Cantonese opera and adapt it to contemporary tastes, with modern interpretations, innovative productions, and collaborations with other art forms such as dance, theater, and multimedia. By embracing innovation while honoring tradition, Cantonese opera continues to captivate audiences with its timeless stories, exquisite performances, and enduring legacy as a cultural treasure of Hong Kong and the Guangdong region.

Feng Shui: Harmony in Design and Life

Feng Shui, the ancient Chinese art of harmonizing energy in the environment, has deeply influenced the design, architecture, and daily life of Hong Kong for centuries. Rooted in the belief that the arrangement of spaces and objects can affect the flow of energy, or chi, Feng Shui seeks to create balance, harmony, and prosperity in the built environment and in people's lives.

In Hong Kong, Feng Shui principles are integrated into all aspects of urban planning and design, from the layout of buildings and streets to the placement of furniture and decor in homes and offices. Architects and developers often consult Feng Shui masters to ensure that new construction projects are aligned with auspicious energy flows and adhere to principles of balance and symmetry. For example, buildings may be oriented to face certain directions, such as south for prosperity or east for health, while entrances, windows, and interior layouts are carefully arranged to optimize energy flow and create a sense of harmony.

In addition to its influence on architecture and design, Feng Shui also plays a significant role in the daily lives of Hong Kong residents, who often consult Feng Shui practitioners for guidance on matters such as home layout, business decisions, and personal well-being. Feng Shui principles are applied to everything from the arrangement of furniture and household items to the selection of auspicious dates for weddings, business openings, and other important events. Many people believe that by following Feng Shui guidelines, they can attract positive energy, prosperity, and good fortune into their lives.

One of the most iconic examples of Feng Shui in Hong Kong is the layout of Victoria Harbour, which is believed to resemble the shape of a dragon, a powerful symbol of strength, prosperity, and good fortune in Chinese culture. The placement of buildings along the harborfront, such as the Bank of China Tower and the International Commerce Centre, is carefully aligned with Feng Shui principles to harness the positive energy of the dragon and enhance the city's prosperity and success.

Feng Shui is also evident in the design of public spaces and landmarks throughout Hong Kong, such as parks, temples, and gardens, which are carefully situated and landscaped to create a harmonious balance between natural and man-made elements. For example, the Chi Lin Nunnery and Nan Lian Garden in Kowloon are designed according to Feng Shui principles, with tranquil ponds, lush greenery, and traditional Chinese architecture that create a serene and harmonious environment for meditation and contemplation.

Overall, Feng Shui is an integral part of Hong Kong's cultural heritage and urban fabric, influencing everything from architecture and design to daily rituals and beliefs. Whether you're admiring the skyline from Victoria Harbour, strolling through a traditional garden, or arranging furniture in your home, the principles of Feng Shui are woven into the fabric of life in Hong Kong, shaping the city's physical environment and spiritual landscape in profound and meaningful ways.

Chinese New Year: The Biggest Celebration

Chinese New Year, also known as the Lunar New Year or Spring Festival, is the most significant and widely celebrated holiday in Hong Kong and many other parts of Asia. It marks the beginning of the lunar new year according to the traditional Chinese calendar and is a time of family reunions, feasting, and cultural traditions that date back thousands of years.

Preparations for Chinese New Year begin weeks in advance, with families cleaning their homes to sweep away any bad luck and make way for good fortune in the coming year. This tradition, known as "spring cleaning," is believed to remove any negative energy and create a fresh start for the new year. Homes are decorated with red lanterns, couplets, and paper cuttings, which symbolize happiness, prosperity, and good luck.

The highlight of Chinese New Year celebrations is the reunion dinner, which takes place on the eve of the lunar new year and brings together family members from near and far to share a festive meal. Traditional dishes such as dumplings, fish, and longevity noodles are served, each with symbolic meanings of prosperity, abundance, and longevity. After dinner, families gather to watch the annual CCTV New Year's Gala on television, which features music, dance, and entertainment acts from across China. On the first day of the lunar new year, Hong Kong erupts in a riot of color, noise, and festivities as people take to the streets to usher in the new year with joy and enthusiasm. Lion and dragon dances, firecrackers, and parades fill the air with excitement, while traditional rituals such as visiting temples, paying respects to ancestors, and giving red envelopes filled with money to children are observed.

Throughout the 15-day celebration, Hong Kong hosts a variety of cultural events and activities, including flower markets, temple fairs, and lantern displays, which attract millions of visitors from around the world. The city's streets are adorned with festive decorations, including lanterns, banners, and giant inflatable figures representing the zodiac animal of the year.

One of the most iconic symbols of Chinese New Year is the lion dance, which is performed by martial artists dressed in colorful lion costumes to ward off evil spirits and bring good luck and prosperity. Lion dance troupes can be seen performing at temples, shopping malls, and other public venues throughout the holiday season, delighting spectators with their acrobatic feats and rhythmic drumming.

In addition to traditional customs and rituals, Chinese New Year in Hong Kong also incorporates modern elements such as fireworks displays, concerts, and international food festivals, reflecting the city's cosmopolitan character and dynamic spirit. Whether you're watching the fireworks over Victoria Harbour, exploring the bustling streets of Chinatown, or sampling festive treats at a night market, Chinese New Year in Hong Kong is a celebration of culture, tradition, and community that brings people together in joyous harmony.

Dragon Boat Festival: Racing on the Water

The Dragon Boat Festival, also known as Duanwu Festival, is a traditional Chinese holiday celebrated on the fifth day of the fifth month of the lunar calendar, which usually falls in June on the Gregorian calendar. It's a vibrant and exhilarating event that commemorates the life and death of the ancient Chinese poet and minister Qu Yuan. Legend has it that Qu Yuan drowned himself in the Miluo River in protest against government corruption, and local villagers raced their boats to save him and prevent fish and water creatures from consuming his body.

Today, the Dragon Boat Festival is celebrated with dragon boat races, cultural performances, and traditional rituals in Hong Kong and other parts of the world with Chinese communities. The centerpiece of the festival is the dragon boat race, where teams of paddlers row dragon-shaped boats decorated with colorful designs and dragon heads and tails.

Dragon boat races are held in various locations throughout Hong Kong, including Victoria Harbour, Stanley, and Sai Kung, attracting thousands of spectators who gather to cheer on the teams and enjoy the festive atmosphere. The races are accompanied by drummers who beat rhythmic patterns to synchronize the paddlers' strokes and create an electrifying energy that fills the air.

In addition to the races, the Dragon Boat Festival is also celebrated with a variety of cultural activities and traditions. One of the most popular customs is the eating of zongzi, pyramid-shaped dumplings made of glutinous rice wrapped in bamboo leaves and filled with sweet or savory ingredients such as pork, mushrooms, and chestnuts. Zongzi are eaten as a symbol of good luck and protection against evil spirits.

Another tradition associated with the Dragon Boat Festival is the hanging of calamus and moxa leaves, which are believed to ward off evil spirits and promote health and well-being. People also engage in other customs such as wearing sachets filled with aromatic herbs, drinking realgar wine, and playing traditional games like cuju, a form of Chinese football.

The Dragon Boat Festival is not only a time for celebration and cultural heritage but also a reflection of the resilience and spirit of the Chinese people. It brings communities together to honor tradition, strengthen bonds, and create lasting memories that endure for generations. Whether you're watching the exhilarating dragon boat races, savoring delicious zongzi, or participating in age-old customs, the Dragon Boat Festival is a vibrant and unforgettable experience that celebrates the rich cultural heritage of Hong Kong and the Chinese people.

Mid-Autumn Festival: Mooncakes and Lanterns

The Mid-Autumn Festival, also known as the Mooncake Festival, is one of the most cherished and widely celebrated festivals in Hong Kong and many other parts of Asia. It falls on the 15th day of the eighth month of the lunar calendar, usually in September or October on the Gregorian calendar, when the moon is at its fullest and brightest.

The festival has its roots in ancient Chinese mythology and folklore, with traditions dating back over 3,000 years. It is a time for families to come together, give thanks for the harvest, and celebrate the beauty of the moon. One of the most iconic symbols of the Mid-Autumn Festival is the mooncake, a dense pastry filled with sweet or savory fillings such as lotus seed paste, red bean paste, or salted egg yolks.

Mooncakes are traditionally eaten during the Mid-Autumn Festival as a symbol of reunion and togetherness. They are often given as gifts to friends, family members, and business associates as a gesture of goodwill and appreciation. Mooncakes come in a variety of shapes, sizes, and flavors, with intricate designs and patterns stamped on the top to signify prosperity and good fortune. In addition to mooncakes, another hallmark of the Mid-Autumn Festival is the tradition of carrying lanterns and participating in lantern processions. Children and adults alike carry colorful lanterns shaped like animals, flowers, and mythical creatures as they parade through the streets, creating a magical and enchanting atmosphere. The origins of the lantern procession date back to ancient times when people would light lanterns to worship the moon and pray for good fortune and blessings. Today, lantern processions are a beloved tradition that brings communities together to celebrate the beauty of the moon and enjoy the company of loved ones under its luminous glow.

The Mid-Autumn Festival is also celebrated with a variety of cultural activities and rituals, including the lighting of incense, the burning of offerings, and the recitation of poems and songs dedicated to the moon. In Hong Kong, public parks, gardens, and waterfronts are illuminated with colorful lantern displays, creating a stunning backdrop for outdoor concerts, performances, and festivities.

One of the most iconic events of the Mid-Autumn Festival in Hong Kong is the Tai Hang Fire Dragon Dance, a centuries-old tradition that takes place in the Tai Hang neighborhood of Causeway Bay. The dance features a 67-meter-long dragon made of straw and incense sticks, which is paraded through the streets accompanied by drummers, dancers, and performers dressed in traditional costumes.

Overall, the Mid-Autumn Festival is a time of joy, gratitude, and celebration that brings communities together to honor tradition, strengthen bonds, and create lasting memories. Whether you're enjoying the sweet taste of mooncakes, marveling at the beauty of lanterns, or joining in the festivities of a dragon dance, the Mid-Autumn Festival is a magical and enchanting experience that celebrates the rich cultural heritage of Hong Kong and the Chinese people.

Ghost Festival: Honoring the Ancestors

The Ghost Festival, also known as Hungry Ghost Festival, is an important tradition observed in Hong Kong and many other parts of Asia. It typically falls on the 15th day of the seventh lunar month, which usually occurs in August on the Gregorian calendar. The festival is rooted in Taoist and Buddhist beliefs and is a time for people to honor and remember their deceased ancestors and loved ones.

During the Ghost Festival, it is believed that the gates of the underworld are opened, allowing spirits to roam freely among the living. To appease and honor these wandering spirits, families set up elaborate altars in their homes with offerings of food, fruit, and incense. These offerings are meant to provide comfort and sustenance to the spirits and to show respect for their ancestors.

One of the most important rituals of the Ghost Festival is the burning of joss paper, also known as "spirit money" or "ghost money." Joss paper is intricately folded and decorated paper that is burned as an offering to the spirits, symbolizing wealth and prosperity in the afterlife. It is believed that burning joss paper will ensure that the spirits have everything they need in the afterlife and will bring good fortune to the living.

In addition to household offerings, communities also hold public ceremonies and performances to honor the spirits during the Ghost Festival. These may include

Chinese opera performances, puppet shows, and processions through the streets. The goal of these events is to entertain the spirits and to provide them with opportunities for redemption and salvation.

One of the most iconic traditions of the Ghost Festival is the floating of lanterns and boats on bodies of water such as rivers, lakes, and seas. This ritual, known as "floating lanterns," is believed to guide the spirits back to the underworld and to bring blessings and good luck to the living. People often write messages or prayers on the lanterns before releasing them into the water.

The Ghost Festival is also associated with various superstitions and taboos, such as avoiding swimming or going out at night to prevent encounters with malevolent spirits. It is believed that during the Ghost Festival, spirits may linger on earth seeking revenge or causing mischief, so people take precautions to protect themselves and their families.

Overall, the Ghost Festival is a time of reflection, reverence, and remembrance that brings communities together to honor the spirits of the deceased. It is a deeply rooted tradition that underscores the importance of filial piety, respect for ancestors, and the belief in the afterlife. Whether participating in household rituals, attending public ceremonies, or floating lanterns on the water, the Ghost Festival is a solemn and poignant occasion that serves as a reminder of the interconnectedness between the living and the dead.

Language and Linguistic Diversity: Cantonese and Beyond

Language and linguistic diversity in Hong Kong reflect the city's rich cultural heritage and complex history. At the heart of Hong Kong's linguistic landscape is Cantonese, a variety of Chinese spoken by the majority of the population. Cantonese is known for its unique pronunciation, vocabulary, and grammar, which distinguish it from other Chinese dialects such as Mandarin. It serves as the primary language of communication in everyday life, business, and social interactions among Hong Kong residents.

Cantonese is not only spoken in Hong Kong but also in other parts of the Guangdong province and among Chinese communities worldwide. Its influence extends beyond spoken language to include literature, music, film, and other cultural expressions that celebrate the vibrancy and vitality of Cantonese culture.

Despite the dominance of Cantonese, Hong Kong is a linguistically diverse city with a wide range of languages and dialects spoken by its multicultural population. English, as the official second language of Hong Kong, plays a significant role in education, government, and business, reflecting the city's colonial history and global outlook. Many Hong Kong residents are bilingual or multilingual, proficient in both Cantonese and English, and often other languages such as Mandarin, Japanese, or Korean.

In addition to Cantonese and English, Hong Kong is home to diverse ethnic communities that speak their own languages and dialects, including Hokkien, Hakka, and Teochew, among others. These languages reflect the diverse origins and migration patterns of Hong Kong's population, with roots in mainland China, Southeast Asia, and beyond.

The linguistic landscape of Hong Kong is further enriched by the presence of non-Chinese languages spoken by expatriate communities and immigrant groups from around the world. These include languages such as Tagalog, Bahasa Indonesia, Urdu, and Nepali, which contribute to the city's cultural diversity and global character.

Hong Kong's linguistic diversity is also reflected in its signage, media, and public spaces, where multiple languages and scripts coexist side by side. Street signs, advertisements, and public announcements are often bilingual or multilingual, catering to the diverse linguistic needs of the population.

While Cantonese remains the dominant language in Hong Kong, there are ongoing debates and discussions about language policy, language education, and language rights in the city. Issues such as language preservation, language revitalization, and linguistic identity are important topics of discourse among linguists, educators, policymakers, and community members.

Overall, language and linguistic diversity are integral aspects of Hong Kong's identity and culture, reflecting its unique blend of history, heritage, and global influence. From Cantonese to English, and from Hokkien to Urdu, the languages spoken in Hong Kong contribute to the city's vibrancy, dynamism, and multiculturalism, making it a truly cosmopolitan and inclusive metropolis.

Learning Cantonese: Essential Phrases and Etiquette

Learning Cantonese can be an enriching and rewarding experience for anyone interested in immersing themselves in the vibrant culture and daily life of Hong Kong. As the primary language spoken by the majority of the population, Cantonese serves as a gateway to deeper connections with locals, better understanding of local customs, and enhanced travel experiences throughout the region.

One of the first steps in learning Cantonese is familiarizing oneself with essential phrases for everyday communication. Greetings such as "nei hou" (你好), meaning "hello," and "m goi" (唔該), meaning "thank you," are commonly used in social interactions and demonstrate respect and politeness. Learning to say "please" and "excuse me" in Cantonese, which are "qing" (請) and "m goi" respectively, can also go a long way in showing courtesy and consideration.

Mastering basic conversational phrases is essential for navigating daily interactions, such as asking for directions, ordering food at restaurants, and engaging in small talk with locals. Phrases like "ngo sik dou ge" (我食咗咩嘢), meaning "What did I eat?" and "ngo wui di ge" (我想啲咩), meaning "What do I want?" can be useful in various contexts, from discussing meals to expressing preferences.

Understanding Cantonese etiquette is another important aspect of language learning, as it helps individuals navigate social norms and cultural expectations. For example, addressing people with appropriate titles and honorifics, such as "sir" or "madam," demonstrates respect and deference. Similarly, using polite language and gestures, such as bowing or nodding, can convey sincerity and goodwill in interactions.

Pronunciation is key to mastering Cantonese, as it is a tonal language with nine distinct tones that convey different meanings. Learning to distinguish between tones and practicing correct pronunciation is essential for effective communication and avoiding misunderstandings. Additionally, paying attention to intonation and rhythm can help learners sound more natural and fluent in their speech.

Immersion is often cited as one of the most effective ways to learn Cantonese, as it provides opportunities for real-life practice and exposure to authentic language use. Engaging with native speakers, participating in language exchange programs, and immersing oneself in Cantonese-speaking environments, such as markets, restaurants, and cultural events, can accelerate learning and enhance fluency.

In addition to formal language classes and textbooks, there are also numerous resources available for learning Cantonese online, including language learning apps, podcasts, and websites. These resources offer a flexible and accessible way to practice vocabulary, grammar, and listening comprehension at your own pace.

Ultimately, learning Cantonese is a journey of exploration and discovery that opens doors to new experiences, friendships, and cultural insights. By embracing the language and etiquette of Cantonese-speaking communities, learners can deepen their understanding of Hong Kong's rich cultural heritage and forge meaningful connections with locals in the city and beyond.

English in Hong Kong: Language of Business and Administration

English holds significant importance in Hong Kong as the language of business, administration, and higher education. As a former British colony, Hong Kong's colonial history has left a lasting legacy, with English firmly embedded in various aspects of society. Today, English proficiency is considered a valuable skill and is widely used in professional settings, government offices, and international organizations.

In the realm of business, English serves as the lingua franca for communication among multinational corporations, local enterprises, and foreign investors. Many business transactions, negotiations, and meetings are conducted in English, reflecting Hong Kong's status as a global financial hub and trading center. English proficiency is often a prerequisite for employment in industries such as finance, banking, and professional services, where communication with international clients and partners is common.

In addition to business, English plays a crucial role in government and administration in Hong Kong. While Cantonese is the primary language of communication among local residents, English is used extensively in official documents, legal proceedings, and government publications. Government officials and civil servants are expected to have a high level of English proficiency to effectively engage with the international community and uphold Hong Kong's reputation as a global city.

English is also the medium of instruction in many schools and universities in Hong Kong, particularly at the tertiary level. Institutions such as the University of Hong Kong, the Chinese University of Hong Kong, and the Hong Kong Polytechnic University offer courses and programs taught entirely in English, attracting students from around the world seeking quality education in a multicultural environment.

Furthermore, English proficiency is a key factor in Hong Kong's competitiveness in the global market. The ability to communicate fluently in English enhances the city's attractiveness to foreign investors, multinational companies, and expatriate professionals looking to establish a presence in Asia. It also facilitates cross-border collaborations and partnerships with neighboring regions such as mainland China and Southeast Asia.

Despite its widespread use, English in Hong Kong is not without its challenges. The city's bilingual education system, which promotes proficiency in both English and Chinese, has faced criticism for its focus on rote memorization and standardized testing rather than fostering critical thinking and communication skills. Additionally, there are concerns about the growing socioeconomic disparities in English proficiency, with privileged individuals having greater access to quality English education and opportunities for language immersion.

Overall, English in Hong Kong is a dynamic and evolving phenomenon that reflects the city's global outlook, multicultural identity, and historical ties to the British Empire. While Cantonese remains the dominant language of everyday life, English continues to play a vital role in shaping Hong Kong's future as a cosmopolitan metropolis and gateway to the world.

Religion and Belief Systems: Temples, Churches, and Mosques

Religion and belief systems in Hong Kong are diverse and reflective of the city's multicultural heritage and cosmopolitan character. Temples, churches, and mosques dot the urban landscape, serving as sacred spaces for worship, reflection, and community gatherings. While Hong Kong is predominantly secular, with no official state religion, religious freedom is protected by law, allowing followers of various faiths to practice their beliefs openly and without persecution.

Buddhism is one of the most widely practiced religions in Hong Kong, with a long history dating back to ancient times. Buddhist temples, adorned with ornate decorations and intricate statues of deities and bodhisattvas, are scattered throughout the city and attract devotees seeking spiritual guidance and blessings. The Po Lin Monastery on Lantau Island, home to the iconic Tian Tan Buddha statue, is one of the most famous Buddhist landmarks in Hong Kong, drawing pilgrims and tourists alike.

Taoism, another indigenous Chinese religion, is also prevalent in Hong Kong, with its emphasis on harmony with nature, ancestor worship, and the cultivation of qi (life energy). Taoist temples, known as "miao" or "joss houses," are places of worship where followers pay homage to deities and seek blessings for health, prosperity, and longevity.

The Wong Tai Sin Temple, dedicated to the Taoist deity Wong Tai Sin, is one of the most visited religious sites in Hong Kong, renowned for its fortune-telling practices and divine blessings.

Confucianism, although not strictly considered a religion, has had a profound influence on Chinese culture and ethics, shaping social values, moral principles, and educational traditions in Hong Kong. Confucian temples, known as "Kong Miao," are dedicated to the veneration of Confucius and serve as centers for academic study, moral cultivation, and ancestral worship. While fewer in number compared to Buddhist and Taoist temples, Confucian temples play a significant role in promoting Confucian ideals of filial piety, righteousness, and social harmony.

Christianity has a long history in Hong Kong, dating back to the arrival of European missionaries in the 19th century. Today, Christianity is one of the major religions practiced in the city, with a diverse array of denominations represented, including Roman Catholicism, Protestantism, and Orthodox Christianity. Churches, cathedrals, and chapels are scattered throughout Hong Kong, serving as spiritual centers for worship, prayer, and religious education.

Islam is practiced by a significant minority of the population in Hong Kong, primarily among the city's Muslim community, which consists of both local residents and expatriates from countries such as Pakistan, Indonesia, and Malaysia. Mosques, known as "masjids," provide spaces for Muslims to perform daily prayers, observe religious festivals such as Ramadan and Eid al-Fitr, and engage in communal activities such as Quranic study and Islamic lectures.

In addition to these major religions, Hong Kong is also home to smaller religious communities and faith traditions, including Sikhism, Hinduism, Judaism, and Bahá'í Faith, among others. These religious groups contribute to the city's cultural diversity and enrich its social fabric with their unique customs, rituals, and beliefs.

Overall, religion and belief systems in Hong Kong are a reflection of the city's pluralistic society, where people of different faiths and cultural backgrounds coexist harmoniously, respecting each other's religious practices and traditions. Temples, churches, and mosques serve as symbols of religious tolerance, spiritual devotion, and communal solidarity, embodying the rich tapestry of religious life in Hong Kong.

Buddhism: Temples and Practices

Buddhism holds a significant presence in Hong Kong, shaping the spiritual landscape of the city and influencing the lives of many residents. Temples dedicated to the Buddha and various Buddhist deities can be found throughout Hong Kong, serving as sacred spaces for worship, meditation, and community gatherings. These temples range from grand and ornate structures to humble and modest shrines, each reflecting different Buddhist traditions and practices.

One of the most famous Buddhist landmarks in Hong Kong is the Po Lin Monastery, located on Lantau Island. This monastery is home to the Tian Tan Buddha, a towering bronze statue that stands at 34 meters tall and is one of the largest outdoor Buddha statues in the world. Visitors to Po Lin Monastery can marvel at the breathtaking architecture, explore the lush gardens and scenic surroundings, and participate in rituals such as lighting incense and making offerings.

Another prominent Buddhist temple in Hong Kong is the Chi Lin Nunnery, located in Diamond Hill. This elegant complex features traditional Tang Dynasty architecture and serene lotus ponds, providing a tranquil oasis amidst the bustling city. The Chi Lin Nunnery is known for its exquisite wooden carvings, beautiful gardens, and serene meditation halls, making it a popular destination for locals and tourists seeking spiritual refuge and cultural enrichment.

Buddhist practices in Hong Kong encompass a wide range of rituals, ceremonies, and observances aimed at cultivating wisdom, compassion, and inner peace. These practices may include chanting of sutras, recitation of mantras, offering of prayers and incense, meditation, and participation in religious festivals and ceremonies. Buddhist monks and nuns play a central role in leading these practices and providing spiritual guidance to the community.

One of the most important Buddhist festivals celebrated in Hong Kong is Vesak, also known as Buddha's Birthday, which commemorates the birth, enlightenment, and passing away of the historical Buddha, Siddhartha Gautama. During Vesak, temples are adorned with colorful decorations, and devotees gather to make offerings, perform acts of charity, and participate in processions and chanting ceremonies.

In addition to traditional Buddhist practices, modern interpretations of Buddhism have emerged in Hong Kong, blending traditional teachings with contemporary approaches to spirituality and mindfulness. Mindfulness meditation, for example, has gained popularity among urban dwellers seeking stress relief, mental clarity, and holistic well-being. Buddhist-inspired practices such as mindfulness-based stress reduction (MBSR) and mindfulness-based cognitive therapy (MBCT) are offered in various settings, including hospitals, schools, and corporate wellness programs.

Overall, Buddhism in Hong Kong is a dynamic and multifaceted tradition that continues to evolve and adapt to the changing needs and aspirations of its followers. Temples and practices serve as conduits for spiritual exploration, cultural preservation, and community engagement, fostering a sense of interconnectedness and compassion among individuals and society as a whole.

Taoism: Influence on Everyday Life

Taoism exerts a profound influence on everyday life in Hong Kong, shaping the cultural landscape and influencing various aspects of society. Rooted in ancient Chinese philosophy and spirituality, Taoism emphasizes harmony with nature, the cultivation of inner virtue, and the pursuit of balance and tranquility in life. While Hong Kong is a modern metropolis known for its skyscrapers and bustling streets, the principles of Taoism remain deeply ingrained in the collective consciousness of its residents.

One of the most visible manifestations of Taoism in Hong Kong is the presence of Taoist temples, or "miao," scattered throughout the city. These temples serve as sacred spaces for worship, ritual ceremonies, and communal gatherings, where devotees seek blessings for health, prosperity, and longevity. The Wong Tai Sin Temple, dedicated to the Taoist deity Wong Tai Sin, is one of the most popular Taoist temples in Hong Kong, attracting pilgrims and visitors seeking divine guidance and blessings.

Taoist beliefs and practices permeate various aspects of everyday life in Hong Kong, influencing customs, traditions, and cultural expressions. The concept of "feng shui," for example, which originated from Taoist philosophy, is widely practiced in Hong Kong to promote harmony and auspiciousness in the arrangement of living spaces, buildings, and landscapes. Many residents consult feng shui masters to ensure that their homes and businesses are aligned with principles of balance and energy flow.

Ancestor worship is another important aspect of Taoism in Hong Kong, reflecting reverence for one's lineage and familial ties. Ancestral tablets and shrines are commonly found in homes and businesses, where offerings of food, incense, and prayers are made to honor deceased ancestors and seek their blessings and protection. Ancestor worship ceremonies, such as Qingming Festival (Tomb-Sweeping Day), provide opportunities for families to pay respects to their ancestors and maintain connections with their cultural heritage.

Taoist festivals and celebrations are integral parts of Hong Kong's cultural calendar, marking significant moments in the lunar calendar and honoring deities and celestial beings. The Tin Hau Festival, for example, celebrates the birthday of Tin Hau, the goddess of the sea, and features colorful processions, dragon boat races, and ritual performances to appease the gods and ensure maritime safety. Other Taoist festivals, such as the Cheung Chau Bun Festival and the Tai Hang Fire Dragon Dance, showcase traditional rituals and cultural performances that have been passed down through generations.

In addition to religious practices, Taoist principles of balance and harmony are reflected in various aspects of daily life in Hong Kong, including food, medicine, and martial arts. Traditional Chinese medicine, which draws on Taoist concepts of yin and yang, seeks to restore harmony and balance in the body through herbal remedies, acupuncture, and qigong exercises. Similarly, martial arts such as tai chi and qigong, rooted in Taoist philosophy, promote physical well-being, mental clarity, and spiritual cultivation through slow, deliberate movements and controlled breathing.

Overall, Taoism in Hong Kong is a living tradition that continues to shape the cultural identity and spiritual landscape of the city. Its influence can be seen in the rituals and ceremonies practiced by residents, the architectural design of temples and buildings, and the everyday customs and traditions that are passed down from generation to generation. Taoism serves as a source of guidance, inspiration, and spiritual nourishment for individuals seeking meaning and fulfillment in their lives amidst the fast-paced urban environment of Hong Kong.

Christianity: Historical and Contemporary Presence

Christianity has a rich and multifaceted history in Hong Kong, spanning over a century and leaving a lasting impact on the cultural, social, and religious landscape of the city. The arrival of European missionaries in the 19th century marked the beginning of Christianity's influence in Hong Kong, as they established churches, schools, and charitable institutions to spread the teachings of Christianity and provide humanitarian aid to the local population.

One of the earliest Christian denominations to establish a presence in Hong Kong was the Roman Catholic Church, which arrived with Portuguese missionaries in the 16th century. The Cathedral of the Immaculate Conception, located in Central Hong Kong, is one of the oldest Roman Catholic churches in the city and serves as the mother church of the Diocese of Hong Kong. Over the years, the Roman Catholic Church has played a significant role in providing education, healthcare, and social services to the people of Hong Kong through its network of schools, hospitals, and charitable organizations.

Protestantism also gained prominence in Hong Kong during the 19th century, with the arrival of British and American missionaries from various Protestant denominations. The Union Church of Hong Kong, founded in 1844, is one of the oldest Protestant churches in the city and has a long history of serving the English-speaking community. Other Protestant denominations, including Anglicanism, Methodist, Baptist, and Presbyterian, have also established churches and missions in Hong Kong, contributing to the diversity of Christian worship and practice in the city.

Today, Christianity remains one of the major religions practiced in Hong Kong, with a significant portion of the population identifying as Christian. The city is home to a vibrant Christian community, encompassing a wide range of denominations, traditions, and theological perspectives. Churches, cathedrals, and chapels of various Christian denominations can be found in different districts of Hong Kong, providing spaces for worship, fellowship, and spiritual growth.

Christianity's influence extends beyond religious worship to encompass various aspects of social and cultural life in Hong Kong. Christian values such as compassion, charity, and social justice have inspired many individuals and organizations to engage in philanthropic activities and community service. Christian schools and universities, such as St. Paul's Co-educational College and Hong Kong Baptist University, play an important role in providing quality education and nurturing students' moral and spiritual development.

Moreover, Christianity has left its mark on Hong Kong's architecture, with many historic churches and cathedrals serving as iconic landmarks and heritage sites. The St. John's Cathedral, built in the mid-19th century, is one of the most prominent examples of Gothic Revival architecture in Hong Kong and is designated as a Grade I historic building. Its towering spires and intricate stained glass windows stand as testaments to the enduring legacy of Christianity in the city.

In recent years, Christianity in Hong Kong has faced challenges and opportunities amid social and political changes. The role of Christian churches and leaders in advocating for social justice, human rights, and democratic values has become increasingly prominent, especially during times of political unrest and social upheaval. Christian faith communities have played a vital role in providing support and sanctuary to marginalized groups, advocating for religious freedom and social equality, and promoting dialogue and reconciliation in times of conflict.

Overall, Christianity's historical and contemporary presence in Hong Kong reflects its enduring legacy as a source of spiritual inspiration, social engagement, and cultural enrichment for individuals and communities across the city. Despite the challenges and changes of the modern era, Christianity continues to thrive and evolve, contributing to the dynamic tapestry of religious diversity and cultural pluralism that defines Hong Kong today.

Islam: Hong Kong's Muslim Community

Islam has a longstanding presence in Hong Kong, dating back to the early days of maritime trade between the Middle East and East Asia. While Muslims represent a small minority within Hong Kong's diverse population, their contributions to the city's cultural, social, and economic fabric are significant. The Muslim community in Hong Kong is ethnically and culturally diverse, comprising individuals from various backgrounds, including South Asia, Southeast Asia, the Middle East, and beyond.

One of the most notable landmarks of Islam in Hong Kong is the Kowloon Mosque and Islamic Centre, located in the Tsim Sha Tsui district. Built in 1896, the mosque serves as a spiritual and social hub for the local Muslim community, providing facilities for worship, education, and community activities. The mosque's distinctive architectural features, including its minaret and domed roof, reflect the cultural heritage of Islam and stand as symbols of religious identity and pride.

In addition to the Kowloon Mosque, Hong Kong is home to several other mosques and prayer facilities scattered across different districts, catering to the needs of Muslim residents and visitors. These mosques offer regular prayer services, religious classes, and community events, fostering a sense of belonging and camaraderie among members of the Muslim community.

The Muslim community in Hong Kong is known for its resilience and adaptability, having navigated various social, economic, and political challenges over the years. Many Muslims in Hong Kong are engaged in diverse professions and industries, including business, finance, education, healthcare, and hospitality, contributing to the city's multicultural workforce and entrepreneurial spirit.

Islamic traditions and customs are observed and preserved within Hong Kong's Muslim community, with practices such as daily prayers, fasting during the month of Ramadan, and adherence to dietary laws (halal) being integral aspects of Muslim life. During Ramadan, Muslims gather for iftar meals to break their fast together and engage in acts of charity and community service, reflecting the spirit of compassion and solidarity that characterizes the Islamic faith.

Despite being a minority group, Muslims in Hong Kong have made significant contributions to the city's cultural landscape, enriching it with their culinary traditions, artistic expressions, and philanthropic endeavors. Halal restaurants serving a variety of cuisines, including Chinese, Indian, Middle Eastern, and Southeast Asian, can be found throughout Hong Kong, catering to diverse tastes and preferences.

Moreover, Hong Kong's Muslim community actively participates in interfaith dialogue and outreach efforts, promoting mutual understanding, tolerance, and respect among people of different faiths. Organizations such as the Islamic Union of Hong Kong and the Islamic Cultural Association work to foster dialogue, cooperation, and harmony among members of the Muslim community and the broader society.

Overall, Islam in Hong Kong embodies the values of diversity, inclusivity, and cultural exchange, contributing to the city's vibrant multicultural tapestry and enriching the lives of its residents. Despite being a minority religion, Islam continues to thrive and flourish in Hong Kong, serving as a source of spiritual guidance, communal support, and cultural enrichment for Muslims and non-Muslims alike.

Education System: From Kindergarten to University

The education system in Hong Kong is comprehensive and highly regarded globally, providing students with a rigorous academic curriculum and a wide range of opportunities for intellectual, social, and personal development. From early childhood education to tertiary institutions, Hong Kong offers a continuum of educational pathways designed to meet the diverse needs and aspirations of students at every stage of their academic journey.

At the preschool level, Hong Kong provides a variety of early childhood education options, including kindergartens, nursery schools, and childcare centers. These institutions focus on fostering children's cognitive, social, and emotional development through play-based learning activities, interactive experiences, and structured routines. Preschool education in Hong Kong lays the foundation for future academic success by instilling foundational skills and preparing children for formal schooling.

Primary education in Hong Kong begins at the age of six, with six years of compulsory schooling for children aged six to twelve. Primary schools in Hong Kong offer a broad-based curriculum that includes subjects such as Chinese language, English language, mathematics, science, and humanities. The primary education system emphasizes the acquisition of foundational knowledge and skills, as well as the development of critical thinking, creativity, and communication abilities.

After completing primary education, students transition to secondary school, where they undergo six years of secondary education divided into two stages: junior secondary (Forms 1 to 3) and senior secondary (Forms 4 to 6). Secondary schools in Hong Kong provide a comprehensive and well-rounded curriculum that encompasses academic subjects, extracurricular activities, and career guidance. Students have the opportunity to pursue different academic pathways, including the traditional academic curriculum leading to the Hong Kong Diploma of Secondary Education (HKDSE) examination and vocational-technical education programs.

The Hong Kong Diploma of Secondary Education (HKDSE) examination, introduced in 2012, is the standard public examination for secondary school graduates in Hong Kong. It assesses students' knowledge and skills in various subjects, including Chinese language, English language, mathematics, liberal studies, and elective subjects. The HKDSE examination serves as a gateway to higher education and employment opportunities for students, providing a measure of academic achievement and qualification for university admission.

Hong Kong boasts a diverse and vibrant higher education sector, with numerous universities, colleges, and vocational institutions offering a wide range of undergraduate and postgraduate programs. The University Grants Committee (UGC) oversees the funding and development of publicly funded universities in Hong Kong, including the University of Hong Kong (HKU), the Chinese University of Hong Kong (CUHK), and the Hong Kong University of Science and Technology (HKUST). These universities are renowned for their academic excellence, research achievements, and global rankings.

In addition to publicly funded universities, Hong Kong is home to a growing number of private and international institutions offering degree programs, professional certifications, and continuing education courses. These institutions cater to the diverse needs and interests of students, providing flexible learning options, international perspectives, and specialized training in fields such as business, engineering, healthcare, and the arts.

Overall, the education system in Hong Kong is characterized by its commitment to excellence, innovation, and inclusivity, providing students with a solid foundation for lifelong learning, personal growth, and professional success. Through continuous efforts to enhance quality, accessibility, and equity in education, Hong Kong aims to nurture a well-educated and skilled workforce capable of meeting the challenges of the 21st century and contributing to the city's continued prosperity and development.

Healthcare System: Access and Quality of Care

The healthcare system in Hong Kong is highly regarded for its accessibility, quality of care, and comprehensive coverage. As a Special Administrative Region (SAR) of China, Hong Kong operates under a separate healthcare system governed by its own policies and regulations. The healthcare sector in Hong Kong is characterized by a mix of public and private providers, offering a range of medical services to residents and visitors alike.

The cornerstone of the healthcare system in Hong Kong is the public healthcare sector, which is subsidized and heavily regulated by the government. The Hospital Authority (HA) oversees the operation of public hospitals and clinics across the territory, ensuring that all residents have access to affordable and high-quality healthcare services. Public hospitals in Hong Kong provide a wide range of medical specialties, including general medicine, surgery, pediatrics, obstetrics, gynecology, and geriatrics, as well as specialized services such as oncology, cardiology, neurology, and orthopedics.

Patients in Hong Kong have the option to seek medical care from public hospitals and clinics on a fee-for-service basis, with fees subsidized by the government to ensure affordability and accessibility for all. The government also operates a comprehensive healthcare financing system, known as the Hospital Authority Financing System

(HAFS), which allocates funding to public hospitals based on patient demand, service utilization, and performance indicators.

In addition to the public healthcare system, Hong Kong has a thriving private healthcare sector, offering a wide range of medical services, facilities, and expertise to patients who prefer private healthcare options or require specialized care not available in the public sector. Private hospitals, clinics, and medical centers in Hong Kong provide services such as general consultations, specialist consultations, diagnostic tests, imaging studies, surgeries, and rehabilitation therapies, catering to the diverse needs and preferences of patients.

The quality of healthcare in Hong Kong is regulated and monitored by various government agencies, including the Department of Health (DH) and the Medical Council of Hong Kong (MCHK), which set standards and guidelines for medical practice, licensure, accreditation, and quality assurance. Healthcare professionals in Hong Kong, including doctors, nurses, pharmacists, and allied health professionals, are required to adhere to strict ethical and professional standards, ensuring the safety, effectiveness, and integrity of healthcare delivery.

One of the key strengths of the healthcare system in Hong Kong is its emphasis on preventive care, health promotion, and disease prevention. Public health initiatives and campaigns are implemented to raise awareness of common health issues, promote healthy lifestyles, and encourage early detection and treatment of diseases. Vaccination programs, screening tests, and health education programs are offered to the public free of charge or at subsidized rates, helping to reduce the burden of illness and improve overall population health.

Overall, the healthcare system in Hong Kong is characterized by its commitment to universal access, patient-centered care, and evidence-based practice, ensuring that residents receive timely, effective, and compassionate healthcare services when needed. Through continuous efforts to enhance accessibility, affordability, and quality of care, Hong Kong aims to maintain its position as a leader in healthcare excellence and innovation, providing a model for other regions to emulate.

Transportation: Navigating the Urban Jungle

Navigating the bustling metropolis of Hong Kong is a feat unto itself, and the city's transportation system plays a vital role in keeping the urban pulse beating. From efficient public transit networks to iconic modes of travel, Hong Kong offers a diverse range of options for residents and visitors to get around the city with ease.

At the heart of Hong Kong's transportation infrastructure is its extensive Mass Transit Railway (MTR) system, often hailed as one of the best in the world. The MTR spans the length and breadth of the territory, connecting urban centers, residential districts, and tourist attractions with seamless efficiency. With a network of subway lines, light rail systems, and feeder buses, the MTR provides fast, reliable, and convenient transportation for millions of passengers every day.

Complementing the MTR is Hong Kong's extensive bus network, operated by various franchised companies. Buses traverse the city's streets, reaching neighborhoods and areas not covered by the MTR, making them an essential mode of transportation for many residents. With routes extending to every corner of the territory, buses offer a flexible and accessible means of getting around Hong Kong.

For those seeking a more scenic journey, Hong Kong's iconic trams provide a nostalgic glimpse into the city's past while offering an efficient mode of transportation along the northern coast of Hong Kong Island. Trams, affectionately known as "ding-dings" for the sound of their bells, offer a leisurely and affordable way to travel between bustling districts, offering panoramic views of the cityscape along the way.

Ferry services crisscross Victoria Harbour, linking Hong Kong Island, Kowloon, and the Outlying Islands. Ferries offer a picturesque and convenient mode of transportation, with frequent departures and stunning views of the city skyline. Whether commuting to work or embarking on a leisurely harbor cruise, ferries are an integral part of Hong Kong's transportation network.

For those seeking a taste of luxury, taxis and ride-hailing services are readily available throughout Hong Kong. Taxis are ubiquitous and offer a convenient door-to-door service, while ride-hailing apps provide additional options for getting around the city quickly and comfortably.

Cycling enthusiasts can explore Hong Kong's scenic landscapes and picturesque trails by renting bicycles or bringing their own. The city boasts a network of dedicated cycling paths and bike-friendly routes, allowing cyclists to traverse the urban jungle and discover hidden gems off the beaten path.

Additionally, Hong Kong International Airport serves as a major transportation hub, connecting the city to destinations around the world. With world-class facilities, efficient services, and convenient access to the city center via the Airport Express train, the airport ensures seamless travel for both domestic and international passengers.

Overall, Hong Kong's transportation system is a testament to the city's dynamism, efficiency, and innovation. Whether traveling by subway, bus, tram, ferry, taxi, bicycle, or plane, navigating the urban jungle of Hong Kong is an adventure in itself, offering endless opportunities to explore and experience the vibrant energy of this bustling metropolis.

Public Transit: Efficient and Extensive

In the dynamic cityscape of Hong Kong, public transit serves as the lifeblood that keeps the urban pulse beating. The Mass Transit Railway (MTR) system stands as a shining example of efficiency and connectivity, threading its way through the city's bustling streets and soaring skyscrapers with remarkable precision. With an extensive network of subway lines, light rail systems, and feeder buses, the MTR seamlessly links urban centers, residential districts, and tourist hotspots, making it the backbone of Hong Kong's transportation infrastructure.

Complementing the MTR are Hong Kong's iconic double-decker buses, which ply the city's streets with their distinctive red livery, offering passengers a convenient and affordable mode of transportation. With routes covering every corner of the territory, buses provide a vital link between neighborhoods and destinations not served by the MTR, ensuring that residents can easily access essential services and amenities.

For those seeking a more leisurely journey, Hong Kong's trams offer a nostalgic trip through the city's history while providing an efficient means of travel along the northern coast of Hong Kong Island. Trams, affectionately known as "ding-dings" for the sound of their bells, offer passengers a unique perspective of the cityscape, with panoramic views of towering skyscrapers, bustling markets, and historic landmarks.

Ferry services crisscross Victoria Harbour, connecting Hong Kong Island, Kowloon, and the Outlying Islands with frequent and reliable service. Ferries provide passengers with a scenic and convenient mode of transportation, offering stunning views of the city skyline and the iconic Victoria Harbour.

Additionally, Hong Kong's comprehensive network of minibuses, known as "public light buses," offers flexible and efficient transportation options for passengers traveling to destinations not served by traditional bus routes. With their small size and frequent service, public light buses provide a convenient way to navigate the city's narrow streets and densely populated neighborhoods.

Rounding out Hong Kong's public transit options are the iconic red taxis, which offer passengers a convenient door-to-door service throughout the territory. Taxis are readily available and provide a quick and comfortable means of transportation for those seeking a more personalized travel experience.

Overall, Hong Kong's public transit system is a testament to the city's commitment to efficiency, accessibility, and sustainability. Whether traveling by subway, bus, tram, ferry, or taxi, passengers can rely on Hong Kong's public transit network to get them where they need to go quickly, safely, and affordably, ensuring that the city remains a vibrant and thriving hub of activity around the clock.

The Tramways: A Nostalgic Ride

In the bustling streets of Hong Kong Island, the iconic double-decker trams offer passengers a nostalgic journey through the city's past while providing an efficient and accessible mode of transportation. Known affectionately as "ding-dings" for the sound of their bells, these historic trams have been an integral part of Hong Kong's urban landscape for over a century, earning them a special place in the hearts of residents and visitors alike.

The tramway system, operated by Hong Kong Tramways, boasts a history dating back to 1904 when the first electric tram line began operating on Hong Kong Island. Since then, the tram network has expanded to cover a significant portion of the island, stretching from Kennedy Town in the west to Shau Kei Wan in the east, with numerous stops along the way.

What sets Hong Kong's trams apart is their distinctive design and unique charm. Painted in a vibrant red color and adorned with retro advertisements, the trams exude a sense of nostalgia that harkens back to a bygone era. Riding on the upper deck of a tram offers passengers panoramic views of the city's bustling streets, towering skyscrapers, and historic landmarks, providing a quintessentially Hong Kong experience.

Despite their vintage appearance, Hong Kong's trams are a modern and efficient mode of transportation, with a fleet of air-conditioned tramcars equipped with modern amenities such as electronic signage, wheelchair ramps, and audio announcements. Trams run frequently throughout the day, making them a convenient option for commuters, shoppers, and tourists exploring the city.

The tramway system plays a vital role in Hong Kong's transportation network, providing an affordable and environmentally friendly alternative to cars and buses. With its low fares and flat-rate ticketing system, the tram remains one of the most cost-effective ways to travel around Hong Kong Island, attracting passengers of all ages and backgrounds.

Beyond its practical utility, the tramway holds a special place in the cultural heritage of Hong Kong, serving as a symbol of resilience and continuity in the face of urban development and modernization. Despite the rapid pace of change in the city, the trams continue to ply their familiar routes, offering passengers a nostalgic reminder of Hong Kong's rich history and vibrant spirit.

In conclusion, the tramways of Hong Kong represent more than just a mode of transportation; they are a living testament to the city's past, present, and future. As one of the oldest and most iconic forms of public transit in Hong Kong, the trams embody the resilience, adaptability, and enduring charm of this dynamic metropolis, ensuring that their legacy will endure for generations to come.

Green Initiatives: Sustainability Efforts

In the midst of Hong Kong's bustling urban landscape, a growing emphasis on green initiatives and sustainability efforts is reshaping the city's environmental footprint and paving the way for a greener, more eco-friendly future. With its densely populated streets and towering skyscrapers, Hong Kong faces unique challenges when it comes to environmental sustainability, but the city has risen to the occasion with a variety of innovative initiatives aimed at reducing waste, conserving resources, and mitigating the impact of climate change.

One of the key areas of focus for sustainability efforts in Hong Kong is waste management. With limited land for landfill sites and a rapidly growing population, the city has implemented comprehensive waste reduction and recycling programs to minimize the amount of waste sent to landfills. These programs include public education campaigns, community recycling initiatives, and government-led policies aimed at promoting waste separation and recycling.

In addition to waste management, Hong Kong has also made significant strides in promoting energy efficiency and conservation. The city's government has implemented a range of policies and incentives to encourage businesses and individuals to reduce their energy consumption and adopt more sustainable practices. These efforts include energy efficiency labeling schemes, green building certification programs, and financial incentives for energy-saving investments.

Another area of focus for sustainability efforts in Hong Kong is air quality improvement. As one of the most densely populated cities in the world, Hong Kong faces significant challenges when it comes to air pollution, with vehicle emissions, industrial activities, and regional air quality issues contributing to poor air quality levels. In response, the city has implemented strict emissions standards for vehicles, phased out highly polluting diesel vehicles, and invested in public transportation infrastructure to reduce reliance on private cars.

Furthermore, Hong Kong is actively investing in renewable energy sources such as solar and wind power to diversify its energy mix and reduce reliance on fossil fuels. The city's government has launched various initiatives to promote the adoption of renewable energy technologies, including feed-in tariff schemes, subsidies for renewable energy projects, and incentives for businesses and homeowners to install solar panels and other renewable energy systems.

Additionally, Hong Kong is committed to protecting its natural environment and preserving its biodiversity. The city boasts numerous parks, nature reserves, and protected areas that provide habitats for a diverse range of plant and animal species. Efforts to conserve these natural areas include habitat restoration projects, wildlife conservation programs, and public education initiatives aimed at raising awareness about the importance of biodiversity conservation.

Overall, Hong Kong's green initiatives and sustainability efforts reflect a growing awareness of the need to balance economic development with environmental conservation. Through a combination of policy measures, public awareness campaigns, and community engagement, the city is working towards a more sustainable future that preserves its natural resources, enhances quality of life, and ensures a healthy environment for future generations.

Epilogue

As we come to the end of our exploration of Hong Kong, it's clear that this vibrant city is a tapestry woven with threads of history, culture, and modernity. From its humble beginnings as a collection of fishing villages to its rise as a global financial hub, Hong Kong's journey is one of resilience, adaptability, and innovation.

Throughout its storied past, Hong Kong has weathered numerous challenges, from colonial rule to the handover to China, yet it has emerged stronger and more dynamic than ever. Today, Hong Kong stands as a beacon of progress and prosperity, attracting people from around the world with its opportunities and energy.

But beneath the gleaming skyscrapers and bustling streets lies a city with a rich cultural heritage and a deep sense of identity. From its vibrant markets and iconic landmarks to its diverse cuisine and colorful festivals, Hong Kong is a melting pot of traditions and influences, where East meets West in a harmonious blend of old and new.

As we bid farewell to Hong Kong, we are reminded that its story is far from over. The city continues to evolve and reinvent itself, guided by the spirit of its people and the promise of the future. Whether you're a visitor exploring its vibrant neighborhoods or a resident navigating its bustling streets, Hong Kong never fails to captivate and inspire with its energy and vitality.

So as we close the chapter on our journey through Hong Kong, let us take with us the memories of its sights and sounds, its flavors and colors, and its endless possibilities. And let us remember that no matter where life takes us, Hong Kong will always hold a special place in our hearts as a city of dreams, where anything is possible and the spirit of adventure awaits around every corner.

Printed in Great Britain
by Amazon